Advance Praise for

Sacred Sendoffs

"In *Sacred Sendoffs*, Sarah Bowen guides us gently through the loss of our companion animals while also nudging us to examine our conceptions about other-than-human beings in general. After reading it, I find myself living in a more amazing world populated by a diverse array of unique individuals, each deserving of respect and care." —Victoria Moran, author of *Creating a Charmed Life* and *The Good Karma Diet*

"Sarah Bowen's magnificent manifesto *Sacred Sendoffs* is a call to acknowledge the divine aliveness manifesting as our animal companions. If you befriend animals, read this book. If you don't, read this book anyway, and you will." —Rabbi Rami Shapiro, author of *Perennial Wisdom for the Spiritually Independent*

"Our respect for a being's life is intimately tied to our capacity to grieve that being's death. *Sacred Sendoffs* is an ardent invitation to multispecies mourning for our more-than-human companions, from our beloved pets to the deer on the side of the road to the rapidly increasing extinction of species on our shared planet. Bowen helps us explore our relationships with more-than-human animals, unveils multiple layers of animal death all around us that often escape our notice, and guides us in recognizing and ritualizing our grief when animals die. Within this sacred grief work is bound up a respect, a reverence, and a love for all life on earth. This book is a gift to all human animals seeking to live more reverently and lovingly within the larger web of life." —Cody J. Sanders, chaplain at Harvard University and advisor in the Office of Religious, Spiritual, and Ethical Life at Massachusetts Institute of Technology

"Gandhi once said that 'the greatness of a nation and its moral progress can be judged by the way its animals are treated.' He called us to practice total nonviolence—nonviolence to ourselves, all people, all creatures, and Mother Earth. We all need to deepen our practice of nonviolence and help build the global grassroots movement for a new culture of nonviolence. Sarah Bowen's beautiful book focuses that call of nonviolence toward animals. If we heed her teachings, perhaps animals will help us become more nonviolent toward one another—and teach us how to be human." —Rev. John Dear, author of *The Nonviolent Life* and *Living Peace*, and executive director of the Beatitudes Center

"Sarah Bowen is back, and with the characteristic humor and intelligence that marked *Spiritual Rebel*, she asks us to consider the more-than-human world. In crisp, clever language, she presents an elegant manifesto for improving life—and death—for all beings on sacred Mother Earth. You can almost hear her cheering, 'We can do this, people!' Indeed, we can." —Barbara Becker, author of *Heartwood: The Art of Living with the End in Mind*

Sacred Sendoffs

AN ANIMAL CHAPLAIN'S ADVICE FOR
Surviving Animal Loss, Making Life Meaningful, & Healing the Planet

SARAH A. BOWEN

Monkfish Book Publishing Company
Rhinebeck, New York

Paperback ISBN: 978-1-948626-59-0
E-book ISBN: 978-1-948626-60-6

Library of Congress Cataloging-in-Publication Data

Names: Bowen, Sarah A., 1971- author.
Title: Sacred sendoffs : an animal chaplain's advice for surviving animal
   loss, making life meaningful, and healing the planet / Sarah A. Bowen.
Description: Rhinebeck, New York : Monkfish Book Publishing Company, [2022]
   | Includes bibliographical references.
Identifiers: LCCN 2021046089 (print) | LCCN 2021046090 (ebook) | ISBN
   9781948626590 (paperback) | ISBN 9781948626606 (ebook)
Subjects: LCSH: Pet loss. | Human-animal relationships. | Pet
   owners--Psychology. | Pets--Death--Psychological aspects. | Bereavement.
Classification: LCC SF411.47 .B69 2022 (print) | LCC SF411.47 (ebook) |
   DDC 155.9/37--dc23/eng/20211020
LC record available at https://lccn.loc.gov/2021046089
LC ebook record available at https://lccn.loc.gov/2021046090

Cover Image: Vizerskaya/Getty Images
Cover Design: Sarah Bowen and Frank Longino
Interior Design: Colin Rolfe

Some stories have appeared previously in *Spirituality & Health* magazine and *Elephant Journal*.

All Bible references in this book are cited from the New Revised Standard Version ©1989 by the Division of Christian Education of the National Council of the Churches of Christ in the USA

Monkfish Book Publishing Company
22 East Market Street, Suite 304
Rhinebeck, NY 12572
(845) 876-4861
monkfishpublishing.com

To my father, who art in Heaven
And to the 20 quintillion other-than-human animals
who art on Earth

May they be free from fear.
May they be free from exploitation.
May they be happy, healthy, peaceful, and at ease.

CONTENTS

Him	1
Our Dearly Beloved	4
An Inconsistent Truth	7
Pondering Animality	11
Sacred Sendoffs	36
Companioning Animals	49
Expanding Creaturely Compassion	94
Free-Living, Wild Beings	103
Not Quite Wildlife	127
Farmed and Corporate Animals	142
Trying to Heal the Planet	181
Afterword: Living Beyond Our Lives	191
Acknowledgments	197
Bibliography	199
Notes	219
About the Author	237

Chapter 1

HIM

*H*E IS THE first experience of death that I can recall. A shiny black cat with a talent for hunting, he appeared while my mother was pregnant with me. Offering her mangled birds and half-dead chipmunks, he set in motion my dharma as an animal chaplain. My mother began to leave out bowls of tasty Meow Mix, hoping to end the furry and feathered sacrifices. Soon, noticing the new family member, a neighbor queried, "Pretty cat. What's her name?" My father replied, "It's not a *her*. It's a *him*." The cat turned in response and thus was named.

When I was six years old, I also began bringing lifeless animals to my mother. Using my lunchbox as a makeshift hearse, I gathered tiny road-killed bodies, transporting them home for a funeral. I would often arrive at the house distracted by some other captivating idea, thus leaving an accidental surprise for her. "Sarah, come take care of this dead critter!" she would implore me.

When I was barely thirteen, Him swaggered through our front yard with the hind end of a chipmunk dangling from his clenched mouth. Shouting, I pried the critter free and tossed the cat into our house. Although the chipmunk was intact, the little one walked in circles, seemingly stunned. Both my parents were at work, so I grabbed the phone book and called the Small Animal Clinic of the local university. Crying, I explained the situation and was informed that I could bring the animal in for a $90 assessment fee. I stuttered a goodbye, then placed the wriggling little body in my father's hosta bushes, hoping for the best.

A few months before I turned sixteen, Him's back legs failed while walking across our family room's chestnut-colored shag carpet. My parents were at their workplaces, and I was still a few months shy of getting a driver's license. I sobbed, feeling powerless. These were the days before the Internet and cell phones, before you could Google, "Why are my cat's back legs not working?" I didn't even know the name of our vet. My sister, Amy, took the lead, making a cozy bed out of blankets for the struggling feline. We fidgeted by his side. When Dad arrived home, he scooped up the cat and drove off. Amy and I waited patiently, praying, but Him never returned.

He was not the first of our animal companions to die (that honor went to Fluffy, who had eaten rat poison in a neighbor's garage five years earlier). And he wouldn't be the last. Looking back, I realize that we never memorialized Him—or any of our feline family members during my childhood, for that matter. With all my critter-burial expertise considered, I guess I didn't know what to do without a body.

Fast-forward a few decades—eleven more "pet" cat fatalities—and Him's influence lives on. A few times a week, I pull my Jeep onto a gravel shoulder to move a dead animal off the road. Kneeling by the body, I offer words of apology, "I'm sorry about us humans," followed by a blessing, "May you have a most auspicious next life-time." A sign on my car door explains to curious onlook-ers what I'm up to: *Sarah B's Roadkill Ministry.*

Other days, I support individual humans as they care for and then hospice-ize, euthanize, and memorialize their four-legged family members. I ensure these deaths are witnessed and their bodies are treated with reverence. In partnership with the humans who love them, I give each one a sacred sendoff.

And so, you will likely be unsurprised to learn that three cats and my father sit on a shelf in my writing room, though not in lunchboxes. I've matured to using elegant urns.

Chapter 2

OUR DEARLY BELOVED

*I*N OCTOBER 2013, two dozen dogs lined up at the Hartsdale Pet Cemetery—the oldest official pet cemetery in the United States—accompanied by their human police partners. The canines were joined by more than 100 other law enforcement folks and friends to honor Patriot, a 12-year-old German Shepherd. After Patriot's partner, Detective Wayne Papovitch, read a eulogy, bagpipers played. As the casket was lowered into the ground, canine/human duos passed the gravesite in succession, each dog barking at the grave.

Nearby Patriot lies another honored canine, Sirius. His grave inscription honors all those who lost their lives due to the terrorist attack on the World Trade Center, September 11, 2001. Not too far from Sirius lies Robby, his marker proclaiming: "The Inspiration for America's First War Dog Retirement Law." Since the Vietnam War, soldiers have tried unsuccessfully to adopt the retired dogs with whom they served—dogs deemed "excess" by the top brass—to save them from euthanasia. Legislation inspired by the Save Robby campaign finally required the military to provide for canine adoption.[1]

Further along the cemetery path lies the War Dog Memorial, erected in 1923 to honor thousands of trained pooches who delivered messages on battlefields and searched for fallen soldiers. During both world wars, thousands of families in the US willingly volunteered their canines, and some of these animals even won military awards. Yet, by the 1950s, courageous war dogs were stripped of their honors after complaints from the Veterans of Foreign Wars and the Military Order of the Purple Heart. Furthermore, all four-leggeds serving the military were demoted from personnel to "equipment."

In rebellious contrast, a ceremony each June at Hartsdale Pet Cemetery pays tribute to military dogs and other dogs who have served humanity. Patriot, Robby, and Sirius are surrounded by 70,000 lovingly buried cats, dogs, rabbits, birds, ferrets, gerbils, hamsters, snakes, and lizards over five verdant acres just north of New York City. A lion cub named Goldfleck, who was rescued in 1912 from a circus by a Hungarian princess, lies there too. Amusingly, the Hartsdale Pet Cemetery is brimming with countless live animals as well, since it is a certified national wildlife habitat.

Just 2,800 miles west of Hartsdale, over 40,000 animals are memorialized on 10 rolling acres in Calabasas, California, at the Los Angeles Pet Memorial Park. Notable interred residents include film-famous animals such as Tawny (an MGM lion), Cheetah (from a Tarzan film), and Topper (Hopalong Cassidy's trusty steed). While there's no celebrity map available, you might just stumble upon the grave of Steven Spielberg's Jack Russell when visiting.

Likewise, in the Cimetière des Chiens et Autres Animaux Domestiques outside Paris lies another 40,000 animal companions, including royal canines and the war-hero-turned-actor, Rin Tin Tin. Outside Tokyo, the Jindaiji Pet Cemetery offers rows of indoor cubbies where grieving humans can leave vases of flowers and Buddhist prayer plaques next to urns. Indeed, all around the globe, animals lie buried in backyards, inurned on shelves in human homes, or honored in majestic pet cemeteries.

Chapter 3

AN INCONSISTENT TRUTH

*L*EST THIS NEWS make you hopeful for a universal acknowledgment of the value of animal lives, I must now disappoint you. We humans are wildly inconsistent. While some animal deaths receive respect and monuments that will stand the test of time, far more have been—and continue to be—treated otherwise. Not surprisingly, animals living in humans' homes receive the most consideration upon death. Their people will seek guidance on what to do with their bodies. (We'll explore the options they are choosing in detail.) Many will wonder, is it okay to mourn an animal loss as much as a human one? (We'll look at that question, too. Note: If you've recently suffered the loss of an animal companion, feel free to jump ahead to chapters 5 and 6.)

Beyond grieving our animal companions, some of us are also grieving unseen losses. We've noticed that far too many sentient beings are being disposed of—either whole or in various bits like trash—as the collateral damage of our postmodern lifestyle. In the wake of the COVID-19 pandemic, animal bodies were annihilated en masse as university labs shut down or factory farms closed. Human workers were sent home to shelter in place while animals were killed. While the COVID-19 death toll was displayed daily on TV screens courtesy of CNN, the up-to-the-minute body counter ignored the other-than-human casualties of the pandemic. Meanwhile, news reports of possible zoonotic sources of the virus caused confusion and abandonment of animal companions at shelters.

It was not all bad news, though. Due to stay-at-home regulations for humans, some animal shelters proclaimed record-high adoption rates. Social media posts featured workers cheering amidst empty cages. In fact, many rescue organizations had to turn away would-be adopters. There were no animals left to adopt.

And then there's the cat who interrupted Jeff Lyons, the chief meteorologist at NBC affiliate 14 News in Indiana, while he broadcasted from home. Betty the Weathercat soon appeared regularly in the show's weather graphics and even held a Facebook Live Q&A. Or consider the popularity of Instagram accounts such as @dogsworkingfromhome, whose bio proclaimed, "They're the unsung heroes of our webcam meetings and the pawfect 3 p.m. procrastination cure." Scrolling these precious tie-wearing pups staged in front of laptops, I couldn't help but recall photographer William Wegman's 1980s Weimaraners. But, before I digress too far into cuteness—plus a heated debate with myself about whether it's cool or cruel to force animals into clothing—I realize that's precisely the point.

Taken together, these snapshots I've just given you highlight the inconsistent truth of how we treat species other than our own. What's more, while narrowly avoiding a *Walking Dead*-style end of the world, we became more aware of the interlinkage between humans, animals, and the state of planet Earth. Racial and other injustices rose to the surface of our collective consciousness, beseeching us to respond with change. At the same time, oft-repeated messages from environmentalists and animal activists that urge humanity to find a balance between human behavior and the needs of other species became more salient.

What does rebalancing look like? Social activist and political ethicist Mahatma Gandhi once offered, "The greatness of a nation can be judged by the way its animals are treated." His words are both inspirational and aspirational. Because, while we animal lovers may readily agree with his sentiment, the day-to-day reality of living in an interspecies world is messy, complex, and sometimes heartbreaking. On the other hand, interspecies living can also be joy-filled, heartfelt, and stupendously fun.

Pivoting to modern spiritual language, we might call this space of tension the space of both/and. From that angle, we can get really curious, asking a lot of questions and waiting for the answer to arise from deep within us. For example, can the love we have for dogs and cats help us better understand the challenges facing other animals? Can this knowledge help us improve the quality of their lives? How do we survive the loss of beloved furry family members? How do we contend with the emotions that arise from the deaths of wild beings, captive animals, and endangered species? And, perhaps most importantly, can the wisdom we gather help us mitigate the fate of our planet?

This book explores these crucial questions, revealing

eight sneaky illusions we unknowingly cling to about life and death—and how ditching these misunderstandings can both mitigate our lingering heartbreaks and encourage all Earth beings to thrive.

Chapter 4

PONDERING ANIMALITY

*A*s WE BEGIN our exploration, we first need to define the word *animals*. When we use this word, who do we mean? Are insects, birds, and reptiles included? Are humans? And furthermore, what does calling a being an *animal* mean?

Indeed, insects, birds, and reptiles are technically members of the *Animalia Kingdom*. And according to the zoologists who do the classifying, humans are animals, too. So a quandary arises. Because when we use the term *animal*, we usually mean beings other than human ones. Accordingly, some people favor using the term *nonhuman animal* to try to make this point: *Yes, I know we are animals, but I am speaking about the animals that are not like us.*

And yet, adding *non* lacks precision too. A case in point: "Even the term *nonhuman* grates on me, since it lumps millions of species together by an absence as if they were missing something," explains biologist Frans de Waal in his book *Are We Smart Enough to Know How Smart Animals Are?* "When students embrace this jargon in their writing, I cannot resist sarcastic corrections in the margin saying that for completeness's sake, they should add that the animals they are talking about are also nonpenguin, nonhyena, and a whole lot more."[2]

Like de Waal, many of us concerned with the links between humans and other species wrestle with the terminology of animality. And so, we develop creative ways of tackling the problem. Some people favor *other-than-human animals*. Others prefer *sentient beings*.

Lisa Kemmerer, a philosopher-activist who's passionate about this topic, has coined the term *anymal,* explaining, "When we encounter a new word, or an alternative word, our interest is sparked; we are likely to pause and inquire. Ultimately, we must decide whether we will accept or reject the suggested change. Perhaps a handful of activists and scholars will use anymal to replace more cumbersome alternatives and/or to spark dialogue. In my experience, the use of 'anymal,' as one might expect, brings mixed responses but never goes unnoticed."[3]

Indeed, *anymal* never goes unnoticed by my spellcheck, which consistently overwrites my attempts at verbal activism.

Adding more complexity, the commonly accepted classification system that gives us *Animalia* separates us from plants, trees, and other living beings like fungi and protists. For this reason, American ecologist and philosopher David Abram proposes we use the term *more-than-human world.* Abram reminds us that for a thousand generations, humans considered themselves "part of a wider community of nature, and they carried on active relationships not only with other people but with animals, plants, and natural objects (including mountains, rivers, winds, and weather patterns) that we have only lately come to think of as 'inanimate.'"[4]

Eventually, our ancestors changed their inherent connections to the natural world—and set their sights on dominating. As they did, distinctions developed as they created *resources* and *fuel* out of land and made *food* from beings.

So, rather than the result of an objective, exacting reality, *humans* and *animals* are self-serving categories created by people in a seemingly endless cycle of highlighting perceived differences—species, race, biological sex, gender, sexuality, ability, and so on. Each classification we invent divides up the world. Unfortunately, after our subdividing, we tend to place some beings in higher esteem than others. And with this valuation, power dynamics arise. Exploring this tendency to categorize is critical for considering human relationships with other species. Because how we name and classify determines how we perceive and interpret the lives and deaths of other animals.

Why Our Words Matter

SINCE WE EACH process somewhere around 50,000 to 70,000 thoughts a day, efficient shortcuts are a must-have. Thus, humans naturally create *schemas*—frameworks shaped by our beliefs, ideas, perceptions, and experiences—which automatically organize and interpret incoming information. Without this timesaving process, our minds would likely blow up (or at least cause severe mental instability). Reductionism is necessary.

Yet, it's vital to examine these schemas because they cause us to simplify groups in ways that ignore each being's individuality. This process creates prejudices that lead to harmful acts of misogynism, racism, classism, sexism, ableism, and—most significant to our exploration of animals—*speciesism.*

A common framework for what we group as "animals" usually goes something like this: prey, predator, pest, pet, or food.[5] That's not an exhaustive list, of course. Consider, for example, the beings humans use for clothing, entertainment, experimentation, research, education, sport, or transportation. (And let's not forget Patriot, Robby, and Sirius. While some service dogs certainly help humans, others have been trained as attack weapons.[6])

In turn, how we judge an animate being determines our actions toward them. If we call someone *prey*, we presume their life's purpose is to be eaten (somehow ignoring the richness of their lives and internal experiences). Likewise, those unfortunate enough to be categorized *pests* will be annihilated (again without concern for their purpose or needs), and so on with each category. Each word we humans create has a monumental impact on other beings. Conveniently, we often leave their opinions and needs out of our rationalizations.

One of the most damaging words we use—often without little thought—is the pronoun *it.* As environmentalist author Robin Wall Kimmerer explains, "The arrogance of English is that the only way to be animate, to be worthy of respect and moral concern, is to be human. ... English doesn't give us many tools for incorporating respect for animacy. In English, you are either a human or a thing. Our grammar boxes us in by the choice of reducing a nonhuman being to an *it*, or it must be gendered, inappropriately, as a *he* or *she*."[7]

This "thinging" of beings is a learned behavior. Young children often speak of plants and animals as if they have selves to which compassion should be extended until they are taught, or rather retrained, not to. Kimmerer observes, "When we tell them that a tree is not a *who*, but an *it*, we make that maple an object; we put a barrier between us, absolving ourselves of moral responsibility and opening the door to exploitation. Saying *it* makes a living land into 'natural resources.' If a maple is an *it*, we can take up the chainsaw. If a maple is a *her*, we think twice."[8]

Our designation of something as an *it* is our way of being able to act upon … it. Unlike a he, she, or they, *its* are usually relegated to property.

Words about Ownership

Possessive pronouns are especially tricky. For example, are the felines living with me really *my* cats? (Or, as my husband would remind me, *our* cats). On the flip side, do Deacon and Buba-ji consider us *their* people? And how would they describe our relationship? (One guess: That's the lady who can open our food cabinet.) While I have no problem referring to "my" husband (and Sean approves of this term), each time I type "my cats," I feel uncomfortable. So, instead, I try to refer to them by the names we call them or generally, such as "the cats who live with me." (And yet, for simplicity in writing, I'll also use "my cats." When I do, please know that I do so with love and respect—in the way we might say "my roommates" during our college days. I acknowledge this tension and our collective frustration at not having better alternatives.)

How we describe the relationships *between* animals and humans is increasingly messy. For example, while fifty years ago, the term *pet owner* could pass unquestioned, nowadays, the word owner is increasingly viewed as a dominionist term to avoid. For the past decade, it has become en vogue to speak of the animals in our homes as *companion animals* and ourselves as a *pet parent, caretaker,* or *guardian*. Zooarchaeologist Terry O'Connor advocates for *commensal animals*, pointing out that our relationships with animals in and around our homes offer much more than simple companionship. Which is an excellent point. And yet, this term doesn't roll off the tongue easily in everyday conversation. (We'll delve into more consideration of companion animals in Chapter 6.)

The problem with *owner* rears its head again when we look at animals outside our homes too. As a kid, I recall being concerned about the treatment of the lions, elephants, and bears who appeared annually in town for the circus. When I questioned this in Sunday School, I received an answer that went something like this: "God made us dominion over the animals. They are here for our use." I was told this was clear in the Book of Genesis. Alas, my *Children's Illustrated Bible* was quite vague on the topic, and I was left wondering why a loving God would want us to treat creatures in ways that seemed cruel and violent. Was this really part of some divine plan? All of these beautiful beings created and then living their lives out in cages?

Luckily, a few generations of scholars interested in animal theology and planetary ethics have written extensively on this subject since my youth, and *dominion* language is quickly going out of style. Some people suggest the word *stewardship* is a better translation of the intention of the Genesis passage. And yet, there are problems with this term too. It implies that animals need us to direct their lives for them—that they are somehow incapable of existing or thriving on their own. Yet, paradoxically, much of the stewardship we humans provide is required to mitigate problems that we created for those species when we domesticated them. We also fence and develop land which destroys or limits access to food and safe homes for free-living animals. And we replace indigenous plant life in our yards with exotic ones that they cannot eat. Conservationists also point out countless examples of *anthropogenic* (human-created) *violence* that obliterates animal habitats, such as polluting and damming waters, mining, and logging. To be truthful, much of the time we are stewarding animals, not for their needs but rather for our needs. So, humans, in general, aren't great stewards.

Sometimes, the roles we choose for other species imply that they are somehow unqualified to have their own connection to that "something greater than ourselves," which we humans call by various names, including God, Nature, Truth, or Higher Consciousness. Christians sometimes forget that the Genesis passage directed all beings to go forth and flourish—not just humans—ignoring biblical passages indicating that other beings have destinies and relationships with the Divine. This idea extends well beyond Christian references, of course. The sacred texts of many religious traditions tell us that other beings have purposeful lives unrelated to human needs as well as unmediated connections to the Divine. And zoologists have some compelling evidence for animal spirituality as well. We'll take a look at these next. But first, pause for a few minutes and ponder animality.

Reflection

WHAT WORDS DO I use for the "nonhuman" beings in and around my home? How do I describe these relationships? What pronouns do I use for other beings? Are there any words I use which don't feel precisely right? How do I classify or categorize other beings? Am I comfortable with these categorizations? Is there anything I would like to change about the words I use?

Exploring Animal Spirituality

THESE LEXICAL AND ethical quandaries inspired me to specialize in animal chaplaincy when I attended seminary. Chaplaincy differs from traditional clergy in that while a chaplain may come from a specific religious tradition, their support typically extends beyond it. Operating outside the walls of a house of worship or a particular community, chaplains are located in hospitals, universities, fire departments, corporations, prisons, disaster locations, and the military, serving people of many faith traditions and paths of meaning, as well as those who are unaffiliated but seeking support. Increasingly, chaplains are popping up in new areas, from eco-chaplains, who bridge humans and the Earth, to cruise ship chaplains supporting travelers at sea.

At first, people got a very odd look when I revealed I was an animal chaplain. "What, do you have a church for cats or something?" I would respond, "Not yet," and smile. Then I would add, seriously, "But I do teach interspecies mediation practices, support animal-human bonds, help humans recover from animal loss, and engage in advocacy to improve life for the other sentient beings with whom we share this planet. Would you like to know more?"

I quickly found that most people answered *Yes!*

As my passion for this work deepened, I endlessly questioned why our religious institutions seemed to exclude— or at least downplay—the needs of other species. I recalled how at my childhood church, my favorite part of Sunday mornings was "The Doxology," during which our congregation would stand and sing: "Praise God from whom all blessings flow/Praise Him all creatures here below..." My mind would go wild, picturing who those creatures might be. Lions and tigers and bears, oh my!

In fact, I took these words so seriously as a kid—all creatures could assemble to praise God—that they once got me in a heap of trouble. I was on an ecumenical youth retreat with hundreds of other teens gathered for a weekend of fellowship, spiritual learning, and in my case, a bit of unanticipated mischief. During our free time, as I strolled with friends through the town, we happened upon a pet store. Journeying inside, I saw a cage full of tiny white mice with a sign stating *Only 99 Cents Each!* A few minutes later, I had a new family member lodged in the large pocket of my oversized red flannel shirt. A few hours later, I was turned in by a fellow attendee for the alleged crime of bringing a rodent to church.

In my defense, I offered up "The Doxology" and biblical verses that suggested animals had a relationship with the Divine, including Psalm 150:6, Psalm 148:10–13, and Revelation 5:13. Grudgingly, the adults gave me a small box to house the mouse for the remainder of the weekend, and my preacher father received a stern phone call about his rebellious daughter.

Two decades later, as I entered seminary, these early exegetical contemplations were constant companions. Namely, why do we exclude animals—or at a minimum, animal concerns—from our houses of worship and spiritual centers? As I started to explore this question, I excitedly uncovered a longstanding history of religious folks mingling with animals.

Indeed, beyond the well-known story of Noah and his ark, human-animal relationships appear in most religious traditions and sacred texts. The famous illuminated gospels of the *Book of Kells* even include mice sharing a communion host.

Many Christians willingly acknowledge Saint Francis of Assisi as the patron saint of animals and the environment. But few are aware that animals show up with many other saints, mystics, sages, and spiritual folks. Consider England's Saint Cuthbert, a seventh-century monk. It is said that after a dip in the sea, otters popped out of the water to warm his feet with their breath and dry him with their fur. Samthann of Clonbroney, a seventh-century

Irish abbess, was known for peacemaking between the "beasts" around her monastery's pond and sheepherding townspeople.

Rabbit lovers should check out Saint Melangell, who fled an arranged marriage in Ireland for a contemplative life in the Welsh wilderness. One day, according to legend, a local prince's hounds took off after a hare, who auspiciously found protection in the folds of her skirt. Melangell's act of kindness endures to this day. It's rumored that no one in that parish will kill a hare, and for centuries, if one were chased by dogs, crying *Duw A Melangell a'th gadwo* ("God and Melangell preserve thee!") would help the hare to escape.

Saint Roch, the 14th-century patron saint of dogs, devoted his life to helping people in need during the deadly bubonic plague. The *Golden Legend*, a medieval collection of saintly biographies, describes that when he eventually became sick, Roch quarantined in the woods. A nobleman's dog found him, regularly visiting to lick his wounds and bring him bread. Upon Roch's return to health, the nobleman released his claim to the dog, who spent the rest of his life with the saint. (In the not so distant past, we might look over a story of pandemics and quarantine, and yet today, it begs for our attention. A study revealed that during the COVID-19 pandemic, while we sheltered-in-place, 47 percent of those surveyed talked to their pets more, and 44 percent felt more attentive toward their dog or cat than ever.[9])

Anthrozoological bonds aren't just present in Christianity. In the Jain tradition, a heartwarming story is told about the time spiritual teacher Mahāvīra was born as an elephant. When a fire raged through the forest where he lived, all the animals took refuge, packed tightly into a circle. Mahāvīra-as-elephant lifted one of his immense legs to scratch an itch. As he began to lower it, he realized a teensy rabbit was now occupying the space where his foot had been. Out of his compassion for all living beings, Mahāvīra kept his leg lifted for two and a half days until the fire was over. Tragically, as soon as he lowered his leg, he died from severe pain. As a result of this kindness, though, he was born next as a prince.

Perhaps unsurprisingly, Buddhist stories often include kindness toward animals, as from a Buddhist point of view, every sentient being is precious and has the potential for enlightenment. One account reports the Buddha teaching a field of 500 swans, who as a result of living the teaching became monks in their next lives and then eventually became enlightened beings. In another anecdote, an elephant named Nāḷāgiri was fed 16 pots of liquor and sent to kill the Buddha. Yet, once in his presence, as the Buddha saturated him with lovingkindness, the animal was calmed and returned to right relationship with him.

The Rāmāyana and Mahābhārata—two Sanskrit epics of ancient India—are chock full of other-than-human beings, including the brave monkey Hanuman and Jambavan the bear king. As an unapologetic squirrel lover, my favorite tale of Hindu origin depicts the building of Lord Rama's bridge over the Indian Ocean. It's said that while millions of monkeys helped gather massive stones and even mountains for the construction, a devoted squirrel joined in by carrying pebbles in her mouth. The powerful primates mocked her. One even tossed her out of the worksite. Auspiciously, the little squirrel landed into the hand of Lord Rama, who after hearing her story bestowed a blessing. "Blessed be the little squirrel. She is doing her work to the best of her ability. Therefore, she is quite as great as the greatest of you. Never despise those that are not as strong as you. What truly matters is not the strength one has, but the love and devotion with which one works."[10]

In the Islamic tradition, a story is told of Muhammad's beloved cat, Muezza, who had fallen asleep on the prophet's shirt. Needing to dress for prayer time, yet reluctant to disturb the cat, Muhammad cut off the shirt's sleeve. (This brings to mind a tradition in my own home, referred to as *I can't. There's a cat on my lap.*) It is also said that one day, when the cat bowed down in thanks to the prophet, Muhammad stroked the cat three times on the back, gracing Muezza and felines in general with the talent of always being able to land on their feet.

While human-animal relationships are filled with much more complexity than these tidbits can convey, these stories may hint at why, every so often, those of us involved in ministry often find ourselves summoned to bless animals. The most well-known event is the Blessing of the Animals that evolved from the traditional feast day of Saint Francis of Assisi. Each year, in October, Christian liturgies highlight Creation, and priests, pastors, and ministers bless pets. Likewise, many synagogues read the story of Noah the same weekend.

Yet, many of us go well beyond this once-a-year tribute to animalkind. Members of the Unitarian Universalist Animal Ministry offer year-round pet-loss support groups, plant-based potlucks, movie discussions, and other events. Buddhist authors and teachers provide guidance for using animal-focused mantras and blessings to help liberate sentient beings. One of my Muslim colleagues answers plentiful questions about "beloved cats vs. despicable dogs" for people digging into animal welfare through the words of the Quran. And secular folks can join in on World Animal Day to promote improving welfare standards around the globe.

It's possible these activities are making a difference, as I find more and more people are willing to consider the spiritual lives of animals beyond merely the bestowal of blessings by religious leaders. Animal communicators tune in energetically to other beings with the hope of receiving messages about what an animal needs. Many massage therapists, acupuncturists, and Reiki practitioners now offer wellness services for clientele beyond humans.

Trans-Species Religion

Skeptics may wonder, is there any proof for all this conjecture about animals having spiritual lives? Indeed, the lasting impact of René Descartes lives on in this question. His declaration that animals were *automata*—complex machines whose organs, bones, and muscles could be seen as cogs, pistons, and cams driving mechanistic beings who could not think or feel pain—still permeates conversations about the capacities of other-than-human animals. Descartes declared that only humans had consciousness, minds, and souls—which were also his criteria for determining which beings were deserving of compassion. According to him, animals just acted on automatic reflexes.[11]

In the 370 years since Descartes' death, science has

revealed a much different reality. Each living being experiences the world in radically different ways that are infinitely ingenious, diverse, and awe-inspiring. Snails can't focus or see colors. Birds see colors other beings (including humans) cannot. Bats and dolphins navigate the world by sound. Bears and moles rely on their fantastic sense of smell. Catfish taste the world—their bodies are literally covered in taste buds.

Even though geologists have named our era the Anthropocene due to our collective impact on Earth, we must not interpret that classification as suggesting the world was made exclusively for people. Humans make up just 0.01 percent of life on this planet.[12] Things exist in this world that aren't solely for us: stuff we can't see, hear, smell, or experience. If we now know that other-than-humans can think, feel, and act autonomously, why would we draw a line denying them spiritual lives?

Primatologist Jane Goodall is a notable pioneer in speculating on the spiritual lives of animals. Her companion animals, in the wild, of course, were chimpanzees. In her memoir, *Reason for Hope*, Goodall reflects on an unexpected experience in the forest of Gombe, Nigeria: "Lost in awe at the beauty around me ... self was utterly absent: I and the chimpanzees, the Earth and trees and air, seemed to merge, to become one with the spirit power of life itself. ... In a flash of 'outsight' I had known timelessness and quiet ecstasy, sensed a truth of which mainstream science is merely a small fraction."[13]

Beyond her own mystical encounter, Goodall suggested that the chimpanzees she studied also might experience something like awe as well, describing how they moved rhythmically back and forth at a waterfall.

Goodall further pondered, "Was it perhaps similar feelings of awe that give rise to the first animistic religions, the worship of the elements and the mysteries of nature over which there was no control? Only when our prehistoric ancestors developed language would it have been possible to discuss such internal feelings and create a shared religion."[14]

In response to Goodall's musings, James Harrod, director of the Center for Research on the Origins of Art and Religion, studied primatologists' reports to answer his own curious question: *Do chimps engage in religious behavior?* Harrod's analysis suggests yes, based on ritualized behavior patterns he noticed in reports of chimpanzee responses to death, birth, courtship, and elemental natural phenomenon. And so, Harrod advocates for a *trans-species definition of religion.*

Trans, as Harrod uses it, means *beyond.* In adding this prefix, he declares that religious behavior needs to be defined in ways that are nonanthropocentric, nonanthropomorphic, and nontheistic. In simpler words, our definition should not be centered on human-only experiences, defined through human characteristics (such as human language), or based on human ideas about divinity. To decenter ourselves, Harrod suggests getting to the essence of what creates our expressions of worship, ceremony, and rituals, as well as beliefs about what is sacred or profane. Doing so, he arrives at the only requirement for acting religiously: "communing in empathetic intimacy with respect to experiences of aliveness and animacy."[15]

Harrod explicitly states that his definition does not necessitate worship, God, or beliefs, and does not require language. Instead, it is based on actions such as reverence, observing carefully, being overwhelmed by grandeur, and experiencing wonder at that which is "miraculous, non-ordinary, surprising, astonishing, extraordinary, and special."[16]

Those of us who have noticed the trend of distinguishing between spirituality and religion might wonder whether we should be talking exclusively about chimp *religion*. While Harrod emphasizes the ritualized aspects of death, birth, courtship, and elemental natural phenomenon, he also describes chimpanzees in prolonged periods of silence (or dare I suggest meditation?) as well as water watching, fire watching, sunset gazing, and python watching (or dare I suggest mindfulness?).

Are chimps practicing religion? Or might they be *spiritual but not religious*? I suspect this question is simply one of human semantics based on our frustration with what the word *religion* implies for some people who have had negative experiences. And so, I'm convinced the distinction between spirituality and religion we humans fixate on doesn't carry over to other species.

As helpful as Harrod's trans-species definition might be for combating the human exceptionalism and speciesism rampant in our discussions of religion and spirituality, I find myself endlessly wondering about specifics. Does a chimp tap into something universal in her spirituality? Or would her experience have a chimpness to it? And if we branched out to the animals we call companions, would their mystical encounter have a dogness, catness, or bunnyness to it? Or would all spiritual experiences connect to some sort of universal feeling of awe? Language is a barrier here, since we cannot ask the chimp, dog, cat, or rabbit what they are experiencing. Then again, one of the widely cited attributes of mystical and spiritual experiences is ineffability—that which is incapable of being described in words.

Cross-Species Spirituality

Of course, that doesn't stop us humans from trying to put words to other species' experiences and elucidate how animal spirituality might be not only possible but prevalent. Indeed, neurological research suggests that what we describe as spiritual experience may be possible for animals with similar brain structures to ours, such as primates, horses, cats, and dogs.[17]

Focusing on proving the capacity for spirituality rather than the observance of religion allows us to decenter language and cognitive functions, focusing on the shared experiences of aliveness and connection to Divinity that species may share. In *Enter the Animal: Cross-species Perspectives on Grief and Spirituality*, Teya Brooks Pribac suggests that key to defining a spirituality that crosses the boundaries of species is distinguishing between intentional and unintentional spirituality.

Intentional spirituality includes those moments we pursue through prayer, meditation, worship, and other spiritual practices. On the other hand, unintentional spirituality includes the experiences that take our breath away, the moments we don't expect but find ourselves in the midst of, only to add language after the fact as we try to describe the experience.

Brooks Pribac suggests that all animals (including human ones) experience accidental sources of spiritual engagement that we aren't seeking out. These events cause either deeply felt awe or an "overwhelming sense of integration within the self, a deep form of contentment as one becomes absorbed and absorbs the space with its tangible and intangible forces."[18] She then proposes the same is true for other species, "Nonhuman animals most likely do not train themselves in mindfulness meditation. However, is it not possible that they may have retained the capacity to engage in such a meditative process in a more spontaneous manner (a capacity that humans, particularly those in industrialized societies, have lost and now have to relearn), and perhaps to actively seek such experiences, or at least embrace them when they occur?"[19] While Brooks Pribac acknowledges that she does not engage in structured meditation or prayer herself, nor is she a religious scholar or spiritual leader, her observations mirror what I experience as someone who *does* teach spiritual practices from a diverse range of religions and wisdom traditions.

I have observed that spiritual seekers practice not only because the actions feel good but because they also help us better manage our inner experience and our resilience when faced with difficult external circumstances. Indeed, a vast number of research studies tell us that prayer and meditation can positively affect mental health. Notably, who or what we pray to seems unimportant for health benefits, though.[20]

Thus, it seems likely that the human development of specific techniques and rituals is an attempt to reexperience moments of intense connection, awe, or deep peace. The *spiritual but not religious movement* (SBNR) is a prime example of a shift from belief-based religion to more experiential, mystical methods. Many SBNRs undertake spiritual practices such as yoga, meditation, tai chi, forest bathing, or kirtan because of how the actions make them *feel*. Love for sacred texts and juicy conversations about doctrinal beliefs often come later and are secondary. Experience is primary.

Does it seem a far stretch that other-than-human animals would also want to replicate pleasant and meaningful experiences? Consider birds perched on wires watching the world go by from their high vantage point or schools of fish drifting to-and-fro in perfect synchronization with the movements of the ocean. It seems quite foolish to think that these feathered and finned ones are merely hanging out, waiting for food to appear. Mindfulness, in the sense of being in touch with our aliveness, seems probable for all species, if only we might drop our incessant need to declare humans exceptional and unique.

Of course, animals do not need us to "prove" any of this. They do not need our permission to be mystical, spiritual, religious, or otherwise. And at the same time, it might be time for us to haul out the so-called "four basic needs of living things" we learned in biology class: air, water, food, and shelter, and add one more: the opportunity for connection.

Interspecies Spirituality

Okay, so if we acknowledge that animals have spiritual lives, might having shared experiences with other species benefit us all? This is the question that underlies my advocacy for *interspecies spirituality*.

When I sit down to meditate, Deacon and Buba-ji often join me without coercion. Their breaths sync to mine, as our biological systems seem to encourage each other to relax. I exhale deeply. They purr. And I'm not only into cat meditation. Indeed, you can find me engaging eye to eye with a squirrel who is dangling from the walnut tree outside my writing room in what I like to think of as shared meditation. Or singing along with the chipping sparrows, red-winged blackbirds, and white-breasted nuthatches that share my yard. An astonishing number of my students relay to me incidents of their dogs sitting quietly next to them for prolonged amounts of time while they are meditating "in nature."

Whenever people confess to me "I find God in nature" or "Nature is my spiritual practice," I often push them a little further. What *is* nature? When we use that term, are we conflating interspecies relationships into this word? And what might we gain from being more specific about who we are sharing our spiritual practices with, naming them by species? *I meditated with an American Goldfinch. I forest-bathed with a spider monkey. A deer showed up during yoga practice in my backyard this morning.*

These moments of interspecies connection touch us in a visceral way, these moments of accidental spirituality. But what if we went beyond chance encounters—transcended merely hoping other species would be attracted to our practices? Not surprisingly, the Universe soon provided an opportunity to explore this question in earnest, as one of my students asked me to help create an intentional gathering with and for others interested in these types of questions.

William Melton had a vision of a thing that was like a church, but not a church, a place where people from any religious tradition or spiritual path could come together. A place where they could relax, knowing they would not be invited to a BBQ picnic after the service. A place where all kinds of animals would be spoken about and their needs considered as important as human ones. Although for years I'd avoided being a "pulpit preacher," I quickly replied, "Yes! And we can meditate with squirrels!"

An endless list of to-dos ensued as we made William's dream a reality with the help of his wife, prolific author and vegan educator, Victoria Moran, clergy colleague Rev. Erika Allison, a diverse multifaith advisory board, and others who exclaimed, "Yes, we need this too!" We began gathering each month to support each other, taking time out of our advocacy work to fill our wells, so to speak, through music, meditation, dancing, and prayer. Collectively agreeing that the journey of compassion is messy, we witness each other's anguish and celebrate our joys. In honor of our shared commitment, we named it Compassion Consortium.

Accordingly, now when I am asked, "What?! Do you have a church for cats or something?" I excitedly answer, "Yes! And humans and dogs, and last week, a rooster showed up." This generally leads to more questions, of course.

For example, once a curious friend asked, "Well, what's your service like?" Elated, I recited the tagline from our website: "We're interfaith, interspiritual, and interspecies!" She paused a moment and then wondered, "Interspecies. Hmm. Like aliens?" I considered this for a moment and responded, "Sure. If we can find some." Then I giggled. I described how *Star Trek*, *Star Wars*, and other sci-fi stories had been formative in my childhood beliefs about to whom we should extend compassion—from R2-D2 and Chewbacca to Tribbles and Vulcans. "I like to think if the beings flying around in those supposed UFOs we hear about every so often showed up here at one of our services, we'd welcome them."

During this conversation, I realized that while the term *interspecies spirituality* is meaningful to me, others may need me to unpack it a bit. And so, we end this chapter full circle to where we began it: defining words.

My definition of interspecies spirituality is built upon a foundation of *interspirituality*, a term coined by Catholic monk and social justice advocate Wayne Teasdale.[21] And it is distinct from the more familiar term, *interfaith*.

When we say *interfaith*, we generally mean a community or event welcoming people of any religious or spiritual tradition, as well as those who practice independent spirituality. Diversity is recognized and honored, and all religions are celebrated as valid, with awareness of both their checkered pasts and their potential for beauty and inspiration. We seek to resolve any differences in values, beliefs, and opinions through compassion and understanding rather than blame and shame.

Interspirituality is a perspective that recognizes that beneath the diversity of theological beliefs, sacred texts, and practices of each of the world's religions and philosophies, there lies a deeper unity of shared experience. We see that each tradition is committed to common values of peace, compassionate service, and love for all Creation. While each tradition may use different methods, rituals, and words for these values, if we look at their mystical core, we find these attributes. Teasdale suggested that rather than spirituality being solely about the wellbeing of our ourselves, we must engage in a "socially engaged spirituality." This type of spirituality, he wrote, "expressed itself in endless acts of compassion that seek to heal others, contributing to the transformation of the world and the building of a nonviolent, peace-loving culture that includes everyone."[22]

Those of us practicing *interspecies spirituality* at Compassion Consortium extend Teasdale's "everyone" beyond humans to include all species. Admittedly, species is also a human construction and can be a problematic word when you deconstruct it, as some of us nerds like to do. But, as we use it, *all species* means all life-filled beings.

Inter is a Latin prefix that means between or among. So, from an interspecies perspective, we are concerned and curious about the interactions between and among living beings, from the canines and felines we share our homes with to the beings some humans "use" and the ones who are often ignored.

And so, our *everyone* includes the black panther, leaf-cutter ant, barred owl, elephant shrew, anchovy, and golden-crowned flying fox. We extend our compassion beyond those who can't move because the term species also includes the leafy ones and the branched ones, like the red maple, ebony spleenwort, dandelion, and Ginkgo.

Admittedly, all these folks don't show up at our services in person. Instead, we incorporate their voices and imagery in our liturgy. We talk about ways to increase our awareness of the needs of other beings so that we can make choices that create the least amount of suffering for those we share the planet with. And sometimes, we do have nonhuman visitors as well, who help lead us through spiritual practices. These shared mindful moments help awaken our consciousness. For example, meditating with a pig or rooster gives us opportunities to change the socialized narrative about what these animals are for. Instead of seeing them for what they can give us, we celebrate them as independent and interdependent beings worthy of our respect and our compassion.

As people who practice interspecies spritualty, we look for opportunities to be in the presence of the Divine, along with other beings outside of our Sunday services as well. We may meditate with eastern chipmunks, pray amidst the sound of frogs, or mindfully walk alongside Canada Geese.

These activities can bring moments of lightheartedness and remind us to not take ourselves seriously as the beings around us show us what life is like for them. No, not all animals want to hang out with us in the lotus position. While some might enjoy a petting meditation, others not so much. Curiously, my feline housemate Deacon seems to mostly enjoy listening to recorded whale songs! When we intentionally try to interact with other beings spiritually, it's important not to get hung up on the specific steps of spiritual practice—it's the connection that matters.

While in traditional animal advocacy, people may be concerned that animals get air, food, water, a safe place to live, and the right to be free from pain; interspecies spirituality adds the notion that all species should rightfully have access to have experiences of awe, peace, and divine connection. We make space for these connections. We act in ways that help them live long and prosper. And when the time comes that their lives are over, we honor them through what I call *sacred sendoffs*.

Chapter 5

SACRED SENDOFFS

"*H*ELP. THERE'S A hurt cat on the side of the road. I'm on my bike and not sure what to do," Ilene implored. In response, I grabbed a cat carrier, a pair of thick padded ski gloves, and my car keys. Fifteen minutes later, I was crouched next to a small, frightened jet-black cat in the grassy roadbed. Approaching him incredibly slowly, I still panicked him, and he scrambled up a craggy rock ledge, dragging his rear legs behind him. Ilene and I shared a few minutes of nervous helplessness, wondering how best to capture the furry little one. Auspiciously, a passerby who stopped to check out the commotion was a vet tech, and she had a slip lead. While she gently tossed the lead over the little cat's neck, Ilene and I maneuvered the carrier, partnering with success.

The local animal hospital was willing to triage. The vet noted the cat was likely a "stray," based not only on his behavior but also because he lacked a microchip and was intact (not neutered). After an X-ray, she soon delivered troubling news. The cat had a shattered pelvis. While this could be repaired, more pressing was the lack of sensation in his back end, the inability to urinate on his own, and the overall state of his internal organs. It was Friday night near closing time, so the vet offered us two options. The first was to euthanize him. The second was for us to take the cat to a weekend clinic to see if he would show signs of recovery.

I offered up my credit card and selected option two. Arriving at the new location, I noticed the paperwork from the original animal hospital listed the cat's name as "HBC Bowen." This would not do. Hit By Car (HBC) is not a reverent or respectful first name, so I gave him a new one. Little Buddy, or just Buddy, for short, was admitted, and we decided to monitor him for twenty-four hours to see if his situation could improve. Meanwhile, I activated my animal rescue network to look for a home that would attend to his needs while his pelvis healed.

Both Ilene and I posted about Buddy on Facebook. Prayers rolled in from friends for this little injured cat that none of us actually knew. "Praying for Buddy!" appeared over and over amidst copious red hearts and praying hands emojis. My cousin Emma popped in, "Sending healing thoughts and will donate to a GoFundMe to help cover vet bills if needed. Come on, little dude." I lit candles on my altar, prayed, and hoped for the best.

But alas, the next day, I received *the phone call.* Delicately, the on-call vet reported that Buddy was not getting better. In addition, each time the staff had to push on his bladder to make it release, he became more frightened. While most home-based cats will tolerate a little bit of this, the hospital was likely a scary place for a free-living roamer like Buddy. The prognosis was poor, and they recommended euthanasia. Unable to find a placement for him unless the bladder situation improved, I was out of options.

Except to plan his sacred sendoff.

Usually, I like to be present for euthanasia. But, in this case, since I did not have a prior relationship with the cat, I was unsure if my presence would be helpful and suspected it might create more suffering. If the staff moved Buddy to a room where I could be present with him, this would likely terrify him more than doing the procedure where he was currently located. So, I asked if I could email them a blessing to read to him. They agreed, and I wrote my prayer broadly, sensitive to the fact that I did not know the religious or spiritual outlook of whoever might be delivering the words.

> Dear little one,
>
> Please know that you have been loved by the Universe. You have been loved by the ones who found you and the ones who have tried to heal you. From here, we wish you a most auspicious next lifetime. May you be free from pain. May you be free from fear. May you now experience a sacred sendoff. Amen.

An hour later, I arrived to pick up Buddy and bring him to my home. The clinic had placed him in a white cardboard box with a carrying handle. Holding back tears, I noticed they had printed and affixed my blessing to the top, along with a small packet of forget-me-not flower seeds. When I remarked on how much I appreciated this gesture, they inquired if they could do the same for other cats who arrived through good Samaritans. "Yes, of course! Thank you!" I responded, firm in my belief that while I cannot prove that words of blessing help the transition to *What's Next*, I hope that they do.

As I took the sorta-coffin in my hands, I noticed that heat radiated through the bottom from his body. My mind was utterly empty, my heart numb. I drove slowly, speaking softly to Buddy in his box. Upon arriving home, I found my husband had dug a sizable hole in a woodsy area and fashioned a cross out of two large sticks mounted onto a metal pole. Into the crossbar, he had carved a single letter: B.

I placed Buddy into the grave, covering him in flowers, and tossing in a brightly colored, catnip-filled unicorn toy I appropriated from Deacon and Buba-ji. I offered a prayer for Buddy's transition. Next to the grave, I placed two folding chairs and waited for Ilene to arrive.

Together we sat, reflecting on the events of the last two days. We wondered if we had helped Buddy, pondering that at least he hadn't painfully become someone else's live dinner. Ilene thanked me for being her partner in this experience, and I thanked her for including me in witnessing this little one's last day on Earth. After a bit of silence, I rose and started to shovel the loose dirt back into the new grave. Soon, Ilene interrupted me, "We share the work in my faith." Handing her the shovel, I sat down, watching her finish this sacred task in silence.

We broke the news to our friends on Facebook,

and more commentary ensued for him, "Rest in peace, Buddy." And for us, "Thank you for showing love."

Not one person asked why we had buried a cat that we didn't know.

A Brief History of Animal Burial

THE IDEA OF reverently sending off an animal to *whatever is next* is not new, of course. Zooarcheologists' discoveries reveal that the practice of burying animals has remarkably ancient roots. French archeologists suggest that one of the oldest known "pet" cats lived about 9,500 years ago in Cyprus.[23] (While the Egyptian interment of cats is well established, those burials didn't start till around 2000 BCE[24]).

Merely finding cat remains in or near ancient human settlements doesn't necessarily imply those animals were pets, though. Before what we call *domestication*, cats likely lived with humans as *commensal domesticates*, a term developed to describe animals that weren't explicitly raised by people but were attracted to human habitations—such as mice, rats, sparrows, and early dogs. Notably, the Cyprus find suggests a personal bond, though, as the cat is placed within the same grave as a human. Yet, the discovery has a darker side as well: "Analysis suggests that the cat was just eight months old at death and was possibly killed in order to be buried alongside the human."[25]

Intentional burials of dogs occurred even further back in time and are more common in archaeological finds. A puppy uncovered in a grave near what is now Bonn, Germany, has been dated 14,000 years ago.

Dental evaluation revealed the puppy likely had experienced multiple illnesses due to the canine distemper virus, possibly two or three periods of severe illness lasting five to six weeks each. "Since distemper is a life-threatening sickness with very high mortality rates, the dog must have been perniciously ill between the ages of 19 and 23 weeks. It probably could only have survived thanks to intensive and long-lasting human care and nursing," reported Liane Giemsch, an archaeologist specializing in the Neolithic Period.[26] According to Giemsch, this type of care toward an ill animal of no utility to people suggests a bond of compassion or empathy.

If you are anything like me, these early anecdotal burial stories pull on your heartstrings, providing long-sought proof of what we believe: Animal deaths are worth our consideration. Yet, while there are some plausible signs of animals being buried as companions and the human-animal bond has grown stronger throughout the ages, most animals probably were not buried reverently. Zooarcheologists reveal, "the reality is that most animals found buried throughout human history were not buried as companions and were not buried in graves; they were buried in pits and were buried for a functional purpose for humans or were simply discarded by humans."[27]

Divine Creatures

THERE ARE INTRIGUING exceptions, though. In Egypt, animals deemed sacred—usually due to specific or unusual markings—were often kept in special temple enclosures during their lives, served by priests, and supported by endowments and royal grants. Upon their deaths, they received extraordinary treatment prompted by their perceived connection to the Divine. Salima Ikram, professor of Egyptology at the American University in Cairo, explains,

> For Apis bulls, the mourning period lasted seventy days while the animal was mummified, after which its funeral would be celebrated. Priests of the animals, and even the people of the area, wore mourning garments, did not cut or wash their hair, and mourned loudly and publicly for the loss of their god. For the first four days of the mourning period, mourners fasted and ate only bread and vegetables for the remainder. Once mummified, the sacred animal would be taken to the special cemeteries that had been established for them, placed in coffins and sarcophagi, some of which had canopies over them, and had the final rites administered.[28]

Anthrozoologists suggest divine animals were viewed as having the spirit of a god within them. Upon death, this spirit could be passed on to another animal. (Ikram compares this to modern beliefs about the Dalai Lama or Living Goddess.)

Indeed, Egyptians buried millions of animals: Cats, donkeys, gazelles, and ducks have been found in their own coffins. Elephants, cattle, baboons, rams, crocodiles, falcons, hyenas, bats, owls, snakes, lizards, scarab beetles, and even a hippopotamus were entombed.

Lest we romanticize the Egyptians too much as animal-lovers, it's crucial to note that animals were mummified for various reasons—not just to revere a passed pet or honor a sacred animal. Ducks, geese, pigeons, sheep, goats, and cattle were also turned into *victual mummies* to serve as funerary food for humans in the afterlife. Tutankhamun was buried with forty cases full. And while pet cats were usually allowed to live out their lives naturally, many cats—and other creatures, including birds, baboons, and dogs—were bred, raised, and killed by blunt force or strangulation to be turned into *votive mummies*.[29] A robust industry created and sold these prepared animals to pilgrims, who would offer them as an act of dedication at religious shrines. After a presentation to the god, priests buried the votives in massive animal cemeteries. Sometimes their bodies would be taken out for annual processions, then reburied.[30]

The scale of this cannot be understated. Hundreds of thousands of cats were buried in some of these cemeteries. Nor can we naively think these animals lie still interred. Over the years, they have been pillaged by tomb raiders, removed for research, or destroyed by fire and water. Some also met a fate that I suspect would have been abhorrent to ancient Egyptians—and seen as another case of exploitation and colonialization by present residents of the area. "Cats buried at Bubastis and Stabel Antar were so numerous that they were used as ballast for ships going back to Europe, where they were used as fertilizer. A single shipment of cat remains sent to England from Egypt in the 19th century weighed approximately 19 tons and contained about 180,000 cat mummies,"[31] Ikram reveals.

Not So Divine Treatment

FAST-FORWARD MANY THOUSANDS of years, and humans are still trying to figure out what to do with animal bodies when the life force exits them. Our lexical quandaries follow us here, too. While alive, both humans and animals have *bodies*. Yet, upon death, humans and some animals are often referred to as *corpses* (or *cadavers*), while other animals become *carcasses* (and perhaps even *fossils*).

As an animal chaplain, I find that this word *carcass* irritates me to no end—as does the suggestion that somehow human bodies deserve more reverence at their death than other species do. Yet, with the remarkable exceptions that we explored in Chapter 2, that's usually what happens. Consider, for example, what transpired during America's Civil War. As over 620,000 soldiers died, handling and preserving the bodies—both human and other-than-human—created a national issue that spurred new technology.[32] On-location embalming and cooled transportation cases carried on train cars enabled preserved bodies of soldiers to return to their hometowns, which was considered a critical action for maintaining the value of human life.[33]

In contrast, most "bridled soldiers" were dropped into mass graves, burned on the ground, or simply abandoned on battlefields or roadsides. By the end of the war, it's estimated that 1.2 million horses and mules were killed in battle or worn out from drawing supply wagons and ambulances or carrying artillery.[34] That's double the number of humans who died. Sit with that for a minute—over 1.8 million lives were lost in the war, and over two-thirds of them were four-legged.

Eventually, a Calvary War Horse statue was placed adjacent to the United States Cavalry Museum at Fort Riley, Kansas. The inscription reads:

> IN MEMORY OF THE ONE AND ONE HALF MILLION HORSES AND MULES OF THE UNION AND CONFEDERATE ARMIES WHO WERE KILLED, WERE WOUNDED, OR DIED FROM DISEASE IN THE CIVIL WAR[35]

It took over a hundred years after the war's end to officially memorialize the "carcasses."

While intellectually I understand humans prioritizing their dead over the dead of other species and how this played out during the horrors of war, it frustrates me that my American history textbooks never mentioned these four-legged soldiers. Indeed, history remains the dominion of humans.

Recovering Animal Histories

SO FAR, IN this chapter I've highlighted two contrasting ways animal bodies have been handled—the systematic burial of animals deemed sacred and the practical management of animal soldiers during wartime. Now, stop to think for a moment: Before reading this book, when was the last time you wondered what was going on with an animal body upon death? If you have recently lost a pet, that might come to mind, or if your car collided with a racoon on the road, perhaps when questioning what to do about a squirrel living in your attic?

If we sat down for coffee, and I asked you about your animal-death history, you'd probably tell me about the first dog you lost, how the hamster got loose and never was found, or the fish that your father flushed down the toilet.

What's more, you likely have losses that remain unresolved. One survey of over 1,000 people who had lost a companion animal revealed that 29 percent of people with dogs and 20 percent of cat people were not sure what happened to their pet's remains after death.[36]

Often, these are the childhood losses—the first animals we loved.

Reflection: Animal Loss Line

GRAB A PIECE of paper and a pen. Find a place that supports contemplation, where you can be undisturbed for a few minutes and can write easily on a hard surface. Place your paper on the surface in landscape orientation. Draw a horizontal line from the left edge to the right edge across the middle of the paper. Write the year of your birth on the left edge and today's year on the right.

Now, close your eyes and envision the first other-than-human death you can remember. Ask yourself these questions: *Who? How did you mark that loss? If you lacked the decision-making power, how was it handled by others? What were you told? What did you tell yourself?* Record the answers on your loss line, continuing until you have reached today.

Finally, look at the line. Take a few deep breaths and reflect on how it feels to witness these losses collectively.

Here's what mine looks like:

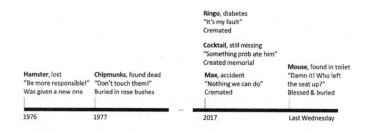

A lot can be learned from looking at a loss line. For example, when you were a child, how much agency did you have in end-of-life care decisions? Do religious or spiritual beliefs influence your loss line? How was the passing of a loved pet explained to you? How did you bury (or *did* you bury) your companions?

Taking Grief Seriously

WITNESSING THESE LOSSES can be uncomfortable. Revisiting them can bring up anger, guilt, or profound sadness. An increasing body of research attests to the pain of losing an animal we are close to, starting with a landmark study in 1990 by pet bereavement pioneers Laura and Martyn Lee. The Lees surveyed 1,000 readers of pet magazines and published the results in their book *Absent Friend: Coping with the Loss of Your Pet.* Over 70 percent of their respondents indicated they were "devastated" by the loss. Yet only 10 percent spoke with someone—usually the family doctor—and less than half of them found the doctor helpful.[37]

Interestingly, almost all the people who responded to the Lees' survey kept some sort of a memento from the animal, spanning from photos to physical items, like collars and toys, or locks of hair. Most people stated they received comfort from these keepsakes.

In the three decades since the Lees' survey, research on companion-animal loss has proliferated. A systematic review of research available from 1970 to 2015 revealed that pets are commonly labeled as family.[38] Strong bonds were not limited to cats and dogs but included a range of species.

It's probably no surprise to those reading this book that many people described the loss of an animal was as painful as grieving a human, especially for people who lived alone.[39] In over half of the studies, people describe the grief as "intense" or "profound."[40]

While most people received support for the practical aspects of dealing with a pet's body, they were commonly left to cope with emotions and navigate grief on their own.[41] Support was sought in various ways, including spending time with other animals or friends and family, seeking professional services, and talking with total strangers.[42]

In the next chapter, we'll look at our relationships with the animals who live in our homes. I'll talk frankly about how we can support them during illness and death—and how to get support for making vexing decisions, like Ilene and I had to make about Buddy. We'll also look at fascinating new ways to mark our animal companions' deaths and honor them. And we'll explore how to keep them in our lives after they have departed from the bodily forms we knew them in. After that, we'll expand to look at other animal losses that may weigh heavily on our hearts.

Chapter 6

COMPANIONING ANIMALS

*H*E APPEARED OUT of nowhere, awakening me from a deep sleep with his mewing. Slowly, I padded across our dewy backyard in slippered feet, searching for the locus of sound. Each time I thought I was close, the air went silent.

This continued for three days to no avail. At night, sleep eluded me. During the day, I was agitated, fearing for the survival of what I suspected must be a kitten. I passionately shared my distress with friends. Intending to be helpful, they tried to comfort me: "He'll be fine. The mom will come back for him." Or they offered comments that further panicked me, "He'd better watch out for hawks!"

On the fourth night's search, I dropped to my knees in the grass, mewing quietly. A raspy, little voice returned my attempt at catspeak. Joyously, I pushed forward a small bowl of food. And out he popped, like a tiny version of Calvin's Hobbes. Over the next few weeks, we got to know each other as I sat quietly on the porch, and he would dash closer on each successive approach. Finally, one day, having gained enough courage, he whacked my foot with his paw as if to proclaim, "Tag! You're it."

My husband took over from there, playing games of *fetch the stick*, like you might with a dog, and yelling out different names for our new family member, who ultimately chose Max. A loveable anarchist at heart, the little ginger feline grew up to rule our yard. Luckily, the other creatures were onto his feisty displays. Whenever Max came bounding out the back door, every tree shook as squirrels and birds sought higher ground.

A few months later, as Christmas decorations erupted in our home, Sean placed a large sleigh bell on the inside of one of our exterior doors. Max soon claimed it as his, striking it fast and hard whenever he wanted to be let outside: Jingle! Clang! Jingle!

There's no doubt Max led a thrilling life. From running at breakneck speed after juvenile hawks to once swallowing a threaded needle, our life with this orange testament to vitality was never dull. Especially the day my husband found Max panting heavily and unable to use his back legs, having clearly been injured behind the building that serves as Sean's art studio. Lightning fast, Sean transported the scared cat to our local vet, who administered an IV in the hope of promoting circulation. By the time I arrived, there were grim faces on everyone involved. Sean and I were sent home for the night. Max had to stay. In the morning, our vet proclaimed there was nothing he could do. Sobbing, we said our goodbyes. I read a blessing, and we held Max's furry body as he was euthanized. My husband and I have questioned this choice ever since.

Interspecies Living

FOR THE VAST majority of us, our strongest interspecies relationships will be with the animals who live in our homes. Perhaps unsurprisingly, our concern for these lives may differ from how we view other animals because we experience their lives intimately. Similarly, their deaths are likely to be more difficult because we experience them personally.

Worldwide, over 470 million dogs and 370 million cats live as pets.[43] Beyond *ailurophiles* and *cynophiles*—cat lovers and dog lovers, respectively—humans "keep" myriad other creatures in and around their homes, including (but of course, not limited to) goldfish, rabbits, hamsters, ferrets, gerbils, chinchillas, parrots, turtles, salamanders, or horses. Studies suggest over 67 percent of households in the United States—57 percent of homes worldwide—include a species other than human.[44]

While ethicists and animal rights organizations point to the problems of pet keeping—including the lack of autonomy and the objectification of nonhuman animals—on the flip side, psychologists and animal studies scholars observe positive effects of interspecies living. By sharing our lives with other species, we become more likely to acknowledge their capacity to think and feel, which are qualities that humans value. This directly impacts the moral consideration we will give these beings. If we value an animal, we are more likely to treat them with compassion. This extends beyond individual animals, too. Researchers note, "If a species is perceived to have the capacities to think, feel, and behave like humans, people become more likely to conserve it."[45]

The noteworthy word here is "perceived." Humans have more genetic similarities to bonobos and chimpanzees than we do to dogs and cats. Yet, we have more interactions with the various species our distant ancestors selected—those that became categorized as *pets*.[46]

A Brief History of Pet Keeping

THE TERM *pet* came into fashion in the 16th century within Scottish and Northern English dialects, referring to a favorite—either human or other-than-human. Its use spread in the 18th and 19th centuries as more people began keeping tamed animals for uses other than food, fiber, or work.[47] Human-animal studies scholars suggest that pet keeping became popular in cultures where resources were abundant, and so people were not struggling to survive. Anthrozoologist Margo DeMello observes that the urge to keep animals for enjoyment is found across most human societies and suggests, "It may be that among mammals, or at least among primates, the desire to share a close bond with other animals not of one's own species is universal, and that freedom from hunger allows that desire to be realized."[48] Once chosen as a pet, an animal typically is named, kept in (or around) a human household, and characterized as *nonedible*.

During the 20th century, as questions about animal rights became more prominent in academic and political discourses, many people shifted from using the term *pet* to *animal companion*. Critics of the term *pet* suggested that it had come to mean ownership and lacked acknowledgment of a person's emotional or psychological connection with an animal.

For example, in the first article printed in the peer-reviewed *Journal of Animal Ethics*, titled "Terms of Discourse" (2011), theologian Andrew Linzey categorized *pet* as a derogatory term. Instead, he asked the journal's authors to use terminology of companionship. Linzey also recommended avoiding words such as brutes, beasts, bestial, critters, and subhuman.[49] (I agree with him on all but *critters*, which I reclaim to imbue with love and respect since "rodents" get such a bad rap—a bit of my own verbal activism on behalf of those living in my yard.)

Beyond linguistic considerations, some animal rights organizations speak to the tension between loving and keeping animals. For example, "We at PETA very much love the animal companions who share our homes, but we believe that it would have been in the animals' best interests if the institution of 'pet keeping'—i.e., breeding animals to be kept and regarded as 'pets'—never existed."[50] As fiercely as I love Deacon and Buba-ji, PETA (People for the Ethical Treatment of Animals) has a point. The way many pets are treated and abused is abhorrent. The work animal protection groups must engage in on behalf of domesticated animals is endlessly heartbreaking. What might the world have been like if we had not brought other species into our homes? Imagine no puppy mills, caged-dog fights, animal hoarding, or mass shelter euthanasia.

Other organizations suggest limits for which animals are fit to be companions. In their position statement on "Species Suitable to be Companion Animals," the American Society for the Prevention of Cruelty to Animals (ASPCA) states, "Species suitable to be companion animals include dogs, cats, horses, rabbits, ferrets, birds, guinea pigs, and select other small mammals, small reptiles, and fish. Where they may be kept legally and responsibly, domestic-bred farm animals can also be maintained as companions. The ASPCA is opposed to the keeping of wild animals as well as wild/domestic hybrids."[51] Note the use of the word *maintained* here rather than owned and the pairing of *keeping* with other species. Yet, this definition raises other questions. How was *suitable* determined? It seems like a slippery word. While it may be suitable for humans, what might the goldfish, lizard, or hamster think? I'm not sure we can ever know. Lumping all of these animals together into a category called *companion* is problematic because it is necessarily one-sided. Furthermore, the ASPCA statement avoids commenting on whether these beings might actually prefer living in their species' natural habitats rather than in our living rooms.

Amusingly, as a kid raised on Dungeons & Dragons, the term *animal companion* also sparks my imagination. I picture a fearsome, four-legged, furry adventurer who has my back—something like the Stark kids' direwolves. But, as a wordsmith, I'm not sure companion animal is necessarily an accurate replacement for *pet*. While I might consider Deacon and Buba-ji my companions, I could debate whether they look at me the same way. Doesn't companionship need to be acknowledged by both parties? Is their failure to leave our locked house enough? Do they daydream of living in different places with other beings? It seems possible.

Now, don't get me wrong. I'm not advocating that households should be restricted to a single species, or we should stop living with other animals. Yet, on the other hand, I realize there is a paradox in my belief that cats should not be kept in cages—and yet we keep Deacon and Buba-ji indoors for their safety. This insight led to Sean building a *catio* so they can get fresh air. Yet, as artfully crafted and cleverly named as that 6'x9' screened room is, for all intents and purposes, it is a large cage.

Throughout this chapter, you'll find me using pet and animal companion interchangeably for simplicity and clarity. I mean no disrespect to Linzey (or others who share that view) by perpetuating the term pet—I'm just unconvinced *animal companion* solves the problem.

Underlying this debate about terminology is something more important than the words themselves. What Linzey and other animal advocates are pointing to is a perceived lack of respect in the word *pet*. And that's something we must address beyond changing vocabulary alone. For example, we cannot ignore the horrors to which many animals are subjected in creating "pets" for stores—caged and bred in lifelong captivity—by calling them *animal companions.* Nor can we ignore the questionable choices that breeders make to increase the qualities that humans find attractive in pets but are harmful to the animals' health, such as exaggerating the "pushed-in" noses of bulldogs and pugs, which can make breathing difficult.

Finally, we cannot bypass the reality that any companion animal is subject to the whims and choices of the humans they live with. The majority of animal companions receive far less care than they need and spend much of their time without the stimulation and autonomy they need. Although caring for the daily needs of animal companions is out of scope for this book, I urge you to learn more about your companion animals' inner lives. (Consider starting with *Run, Spot, Run* by bioethicist Jessica Pierce.)

Choosing Between Life and Death

AFTER LOSING MAX, I became keenly interested in alternatives for animals with hind-end paralysis—because I wasn't confident our vet had provided us all the options available beyond "putting him to sleep." I was desperate to be more educated if I should face this situation again personally or within my chaplaincy work.

I soon stumbled upon Bionic Pets' owner Derrick Campana, whose goal is to even the playing field between animals and humans in the treatment options available. To that vision, he's restored mobility to over 25,000 animals who were facing euthanasia or a life of pain. Campana has treated not only dogs and cats but also a dwarf pony named Lightning, born with congenital limb issues, and a rambunctious potbellied pig named Bert, whose connective tissue disorder caused him to walk painfully on his ankles.

Campana and other pioneers provide technology inspired alternatives for animals, including creatively engineered orthotics, custom prosthetics, and rugged wheelchairs. Helping an animal get used to their new life can be time-consuming, and not every being is a candidate for these methods. Yet, the increasing popularity of alternatives shows a shift in the lengths we are willing to go to help other species. They also reveal a willingness to consider "disability" differently.

Disability advocates have begun to explore the intersections between human disability and animal disability, especially how society tends to devalue beings of any species who are deemed broken or disadvantaged. For example, Sunaura Taylor explores how differently abled animals navigate the world and how their communities respond to their learned adjustments. She suggests that human assumptions and prejudices about disabled bodies are so ingrained that we project ableism onto nonhuman animals, "Many of our ideas about animals are formed by our assumption that only the 'fittest' animals survive, which negates the value and even the naturalness of such experiences as vulnerability, weakness, and interdependence. When disabilities occur, we assume that 'nature will run her course,' that the natural process of a disabled animal is to die. This often results in humans projecting a 'better off dead' narrative and performing so-called 'mercy killing.'"[52]

Taylor cautions us not to jump to conclusions about the quality of an animal's life based on our ingrained discomfort with disability. Because many of these animals can thrive. And there's evidence that animals recognize each other's differences and often lend support to those who need it.

On the flip side, Taylor urges us not to force a "super crip" narrative onto beings either, filling their stories with hypersentimentality. My Facebook feed is full of these "inspiring" stories—beautifully edited with mushy musical scores—and I can get lost in them. But ultimately, I see Taylor's well-crafted point. When we suggest that the only way for disabled animals to have a meaningful life is to "overcome" them, we project human values onto beings without an understanding of what living might mean to them. This *narrative of overcoming* devalues any being that does not live up to our perfect ideal. It marginalizes difference, suggesting that to be different is somehow to be *less than*.

So, what do we do about injured animals or those facing pain from disease? I think the answer starts with knowledge and reflection. As people living in interspecies homes, we need to stay up-to-date on the challenges facing the animals who live with and near us. We must endeavor to speculate not only on what we think our animals need but also consider perspectives that might contradict what we believe. And we may need to reflect further on what *a good life* and *a good death* mean concerning our animal companions. Because as much as we wish to prolong animal lives, we will likely outlive our companion animals. (Although, if there's a chance for the opposite, consult an attorney in your state about creating a trust for long-term pet care.)

Like human deaths, our preference may be that our companion animals gently pass from this world in their sleep, but unfortunately, many will not. And so, we're going to have to talk a bit about assisted death, specifically about *euthanasia*. Derived from the Greek word for good death (εὐθανασία), euthanasia focuses on the *why* rather than the *how*. An umbrella concept, it refers to the act of intentionally ending a life in order to relieve pain and suffering. This good death is sought to avoid a bad death that appears inevitable.

While euthanasia is uncommon and often illegal in most countries for humans, it is prevalent in veterinary medicine, where the procedure is used more broadly than its definition suggests. Healthy animals may be euthanized for reasons beyond their best interest, such as for the "owner's convenience," as a result of "behavior problems," to curb "overpopulation" (such as in shelters), or for animals used in research (including originally healthy ones operated on as part of veterinary training programs).

And so, considering euthanasia—both philosophically and practically—necessarily includes a journey into our own values. For utilitarians, the death of a single animal does not matter as long as the animal is replaced. For people at the other end of the spectrum, assisting in or causing the death of an animal—even when done in an effort to relieve suffering—is never permissible. Most of us will fall somewhere between those two poles. In the case of an injured or terminal companion animal, we will try to balance what we think the animal would want with our capacity to increase our care and financial support to prolong life—which gets messy. Because each situation's circumstances can vary drastically and because we have to make presumptions on behalf of another being.

We frequently rely on veterinarians to help with these ethical considerations. In general, vets define animal welfare according to The Five Freedoms, a set of standards developed initially by Britain's Farm Animal Welfare Council in 1965 but adopted widely since. The guidelines include:

- Freedom from hunger and thirst

- Freedom from discomfort
- Freedom from pain, injury, or disease
- Freedom to express normal behavior
- Freedom from fear and distress[53]

Of course, the devil is in the details (so to speak) as to what freedom looks like in any situation. For example, Deacon asks me for food any time I enter the kitchen. Yet, freedom from hunger does not mean I should feed him whenever he suggests he is hungry. Likewise, freedom from discomfort, pain, injury, or disease does not mean we "put down" an animal because they have acquired fleas or injured a paw. State and country laws come into play as well. In Germany and Austria, so-called "convenience euthanasia" is legally prohibited, but it is still legal in most other countries. (Note: Many animal ethicists and I would debate whether the term *euthanasia* still applies in a case where the animal is not suffering.)[54]

I'm going to make a presumption that most of you reading this book care about companion animals in a way that is not utilitarian. And that you consider euthanasia confusing and uncomfortable. I know I do. No matter how many times I have a conversation about this topic, I never find it easy. And I don't think it should be. Is there any more important topic than life itself? If ending life was easy, I think it would imply that we value that life very little. So, rather than asking how we can make the decision easier, I think a more helpful question is how we can be better supported as we decide.

As an animal chaplain, I am aware that our spiritual and religious beliefs become part of this decision. Accordingly, I advocate for discussing end-of-life care, hospice, or euthanasia with someone versed in not only the challenges of aging and injured pets but also someone who can speak to the spiritual aspects of death. Some religious groups have people dedicated to animal-human topics. (Or, if you are atheist or solidly secular, talk with a therapist or social worker.) I suggest this because, while a veterinarian is an expert on medical issues, she may not be the best person with whom to delve into your ethical quandaries for two reasons. First, she may not be versed in your spiritual tradition and able to answer some of the questions you may have about death. Second, she may not have the amount of time needed for your thorough decision-making process. People who have religious or spiritual questions about death may find it most useful to talk with an animal chaplain or clergy who has been trained to companion others through the journey of death, however slowly that may need to happen.

To be clear: this is not a slight in any way on veterinarians! Instead, I am acknowledging that because we tend to avoid talking about death, we can feel rushed to come to decisions quickly in vet offices, pushing the decision onto the vets. This can leave us open to regret later. Yet, if we've previously explored the topic with someone in our spiritual community, we will likely be more prepared when decision time comes and feel better about our choices.

Furthermore, research on the moral stress facing vets and other people working in animal service industries reveals staggering rates of burnout and suicide.[55] Asking the vet to decide for us may put undue stress onto them that can be avoided. So, while the vet can help provide the details of an animal's health and prognosis for healing, a chaplain may be better suited for helping you align life or death decisions with your belief system.

What Do Animals Think About Death?

THERE'S ALSO AN important question we haven't tackled yet: What do the animals living in our homes know about death? Many wild animals act in ways that suggest they understand when a fellow being is no longer alive. But do animals have a concept of their own death? In 1971, anthropologist Ernest Becker suggested no, stating in his Pulitzer Prize–winning book *Denial of Death*, "The knowledge of death is reflective and conceptual, and animals are spared it."[56] Many people share this assumption.

Yet, researcher Susana Monsó from the Unit of Ethics and Human-Animal Studies of the Messerli Research Institute in Vienna does not, asserting that the ubiquity of death in the animal kingdom and the evolutionary advantages of understanding death provide reasons for doubting Becker's assumption. In *How to Tell If Animals Can Understand Death,* Monsó details animal reactions to death (including chimps, elephants, peccaries, dolphins, gorillas, sea monkeys, seals, dingoes, and others).[57] She then suggests nine behaviors that ethologists should look for to gather observational evidence of an understanding of death, encouraging researchers to dive deeper into this topic.

While Monsó stops short of answering the million-dollar question—do animals understand personal mortality—she does conclude:

The concept of death is something that evolves and acquires more complexity over time. It is, therefore, in principle possible for animals who have lived long enough to witness many deaths of conspecifics, to eventually reach, through inductive means, the conclusion that they themselves will also die. This seems unlikely, but not impossible. And even if it is beyond animals' cognitive prowess to ever grasp the inevitability of their own death, it seems plausible that an animal who has witnessed and processed that several others have died due to a certain cause will reach the conclusion, when faced with that very threat, that her own life is at risk.[58]

Notably, instances of the death practices of felines, canines, and other pet species are difficult to research objectively since they live in our homes, affected by us. We can also be prone to projecting our human thinking onto them.

And yet, consider the case of Oscar, the hospice cat. While living as a therapy cat in a Rhode Island nursing and rehab center, Oscar was described as "generally unsociable" but highly attuned to residents' health at the end of their lives. Time after time, nurses found Oscar napping with a patient shortly before the person's death. In a paper for the *New England Journal of Medicine*, Dr. David Dosa noted Oscar's presence at a bedside was "viewed by physicians and nursing home staff as an almost absolute indicator of impending death, allowing staff members to adequately notify families."[59] For those with no family members, Oscar provided company and comfort to those who might have died alone. Dosa suggested that Oscar might have been attracted to patients based on the scent that dying cells emit. And yet, that answer doesn't quite explain why this cat chose to stay—it couldn't be merely for biological reasons.

Evidence of animal altruism and capacity for empathy has been mounting in the last decade. Combined with research on animal grieving, I think there is a strong possibility that our animal companions understand *something* is going on as they approach the moment of death, whether it is a natural one or as we prepare them for euthanasia. This belief has led me to deeply contemplate what spiritual support might be useful for them at the time of their passing.

Supporting Animals During Death

I SUGGEST FOUR things humans can do at the time of animal death. First, speak honestly with the animal about what is going on (and why the choice of euthanasia was made, if applicable). Second, connect with the animal through gentle touch. Third, read aloud some words which are meaningful to the human participants. People I work with sometimes choose to write their own. (I also offer prayers, blessings, and other words for death at sacredsendoffs.com/words, which might be helpful.) Fourth, after the animal ceases breathing, I recommend sitting with them for a few minutes and then taking the rest of the day off to start integrating the reality of the loss and engaging in self-care.

Humans Need Support, Too

AFTER THE DEATH of a companion animal, sadness, grief, or guilt will likely be present. These can significantly impact our lives. One study found that 93 percent of humans reported a disruption in their lives, such as trouble sleeping or losing appetite. Over 50 percent reduced their social activities, and 45 percent had job-related difficulties. Other studies have documented people's loss of motivation, increased stress, anxiety, worry, and depression.[60] Furthermore, animal death tends to resurface our memories of past bereavements and losses.

People describe their grief to me based on how it wreaks havoc in their lives: *I can't function. I can't think straight. My heart hurts. All I can do is cry. I'm never prepared for when it hits; grief floods me.*

It seems easier to describe what grief *does* rather than what grief *is*. I'm partial to this definition: Grief is "the response to loss in all of its totality—including its physical, emotional, cognitive, behavioral, and spiritual manifestations—and as a natural and normal reaction to loss."[61] That last part is worth repeating—as a *natural* and *normal* reaction to loss.

Even though plentiful research validates the impact of grief, how people respond to us—thoughtfully or not—can vary, especially when it comes to animal loss. Some people in your life may "get it." Others may suggest you "get over it." When grief is socially negated, we refer to it as *disenfranchised grief,* and this seems to make the loss hurt even more.

A Plan for Managing Grief

If you have recently experienced a loss, let me be clear: What you are experiencing is real. And it is valid. And it stinks. I am so sorry for your loss. If there is one thing I can underline, highlight, and might write in ALL CAPS for you, it would be this: Don't try to go it alone. Support is essential. Find people who get you and spend time talking about your loss with them. Google "pet loss support group near me." Or, if you don't like groups, meet with a bereavement counselor, animal chaplain, or therapist. If your emotions get so intense you feel suicidal at any point or concerned for your safety, call 911—*immediately!*

For many years, it was suggested that grief progressed in a linear model through stages. And there is some comfort, perhaps in being able to say, "Well, I've gotten over my denial, anger, and bargaining stages, and now I'm really focused on kicking this depression and moving on to acceptance!" And yet, the more grief has been studied, the more it defies being meticulously organized. Of course, that doesn't stop us from developing models. When I work with people on grief, I draw heavily from the work of psychologist J. William Worden. Worden suggests that grief is not something that happens *to us,* but that we can take an active part in our grieving by accepting the reality of the loss, processing the pain of grief, adjusting to a world without the deceased (internally, externally, and spiritually), and finding an enduring connection with the deceased in the midst of embarking on a new life.[62]

Although Worden focused primarily on humans

mourning other humans, I have found his model easily extendable to animal loss, with some adaptations.

1. Accepting the Reality of the Loss

For our purposes, accepting the reality of an animal loss often starts with dealing with the practicalities of the body. Deathcare practices, including memorializing or ritualizing, can help us accept the change in the physical status of the animal's life. (So, I'll provide a wide range of options later in this chapter. If you are currently deciding what to do with an animal body, skip ahead to page 70.)

Acceptance also requires recognizing what we are feeling and experiencing—and addressing any unhelpful self-talk. Sometimes, the statements that block us from coping are ones we create ourselves. If you find yourself ruminating or feeling stuck in grief, try the following practice:

Grab some tissues, paper, and a pen. Find a safe, cozy place where you can be exactly as you are, without feeling the need to appear okay for others. Take a few deep breaths. Close your eyes if you feel comfortable; if not, just gaze softly on something and let your vision fuzz up a bit. Sit for two to three minutes, noticing your breaths.

Bring to mind the animal you have lost. Write down all the thoughts that come to mind. Just keep writing until you feel complete. Now, look at what you wrote. Notice if your writing includes the words must, have to, can't, should, or other imperatives, such as *I have to let go. I have to move on. I have to be strong. It must have been my fault. I should have. . . .* If you are having these thoughts, acknowledge that you do *not* have to do anything. What you are feeling is natural and normal.

Notice if your writing includes any statements from others that invalidate your experience. *It's just a dog. Don't feel bad. Get your mind on something else. Time heals all wounds.* Acknowledge that while these people are trying to be helpful, their words may not be. Have compassion for them in their concern for you, and at the same time, realize that you do not need to take these statements as true.

Welcome any feelings that come, rather than try to suppress them. Speak to these emotions out loud. *Welcome, sadness. Welcome, anger. Welcome, tears.* Ask Spirit, God, Goddess, Higher Power—by whatever name or concept you use—to enter into these emotions with you. *Support me in my sadness. Be with me in my anger.*

Spend a few moments observing how reaching outside of yourself feels. Notice the place, or places, in your body that hold the sensations of loss. Now, welcome healing into your body and thoughts. Say aloud: *Welcome, healing.*

Sit for a few more minutes, returning to following your breaths. You may find you need to repeat this exercise frequently throughout the day.

2. Processing the Pain of Grief and Adjusting to Life after Loss

Processing pain and adjusting to a world without the deceased is hands-down the messiest part of loss. And as much as I'd like to provide you perfect instructions, I don't think that working with grief on your own by reading a book is sufficient. And I definitely do not believe that you need to work it out yourself so that the people around you can stop feeling uncomfortable with your sadness. Instead, to best survive animal loss, I recommend you engage with others. Because—newsflash!—the process of bereavement will likely continue for many weeks or months. I can't get you "over it" in a weekend with a few tips. There is no prize for getting over grief quickly. In fact, speeding through the process can often be detrimental to your long-term wellbeing.

Research suggests that both talking about our pet's death and social support are essential to the grieving process.[63] While speaking with supportive friends and family is one piece of the puzzle, talking with a professional can also be incredibly beneficial. To help you find support, at sacredsendoffs.com/grief, I maintain a list of support group meetings, online communities, and message boards—as well as suggestions for how to find an animal chaplain or other helpful professional near you.

3. Finding Enduring Connections

This is where spirituality comes into the process. How do we find an enduring connection with the deceased? Many people ask me what I think happens to animal souls or spirits at death. So, we'll look at that question in detail in just a bit. For now, my short version is this: thermodynamics tells us that energy is never destroyed; it just constantly changes form. So, while you may not be able to converse with Fluffy or Fido in the way you did before their bodily death, I think it's perfectly natural, and often helpful, to keep talking to them even though the form you once knew them as has changed.

I vehemently disagree with well-meaning professionals who suggest that the best thing is "closure" for your pet relationship or those who see grief as an unhealthy attachment to an animal, and I wholeheartedly agree with those who suggest continuing bonds.[64] Of course, how we can understand and work with our bond to an animal companion will depend on our beliefs about death, as well as the familial and cultural messages that helped form those beliefs. In many cases, we may need to unpack restrictive or limiting narratives to transform our relationship with a being after the death of their body.

Rather than thinking we need to move on, get past the pain, or stop feeling grief, we may just need to find a place to put all that love we once showered on our pets when they were alive. Because while we may not know the precise details of what happens after bodily death, we can still cultivate spiritual connections to those who have passed on. Talk to your passed-on furry friend. Write them love poems. Make a small altar to honor their life.

In addition, consider showering love on the other animals you encounter—human and nonhuman alike. It's often said that grief is love with nowhere to go. So, hug your friends. Talk to songbirds. Meditate with butterflies. Radiate love to all creatures, always.

Sending Off Our Animal Companions

IN ADDITION TO managing emotional responses to loss, there are practical decisions to be made about bodies. Our discomfort with those decisions often leads to delegating the responsibility to someone else. And it can lead to not being honest with others—especially children—about the practical side of deathcare. Case in point: I have no idea what actually happened to the bodies of any of our family cats during my childhood. I recall burying many passed-on hamsters next to the road-killed chipmunks, of course, but the felines remain a mystery that my father took to his grave.

If a pet does die at home—either in their sleep or otherwise—it is crucial to keep their body cool while you sort out aftercare details. Place the body in the coldest place in your home, packed with bags of ice. Or, in the case of a small pet, you can wrap the body securely in a plastic bag and place it in your refrigerator or freezer while you resolve your next steps.

If your pet has been under the care of a veterinarian, you can call them for help with the disposition of the body, or you may work directly with a pet cemetery, crematorium, or other deathcare provider. (We'll talk more about these options in a bit.)

While state laws about the disposition of human bodies are common, regulations regarding animal bodies are haphazard at best. Families are regularly under-informed by veterinarians about the choices they have for aftercare because we are afraid—or too distressed—to ask. So, let me be clear: You have a right to ask your vet about the options available and to ask as many questions as you need to until you understand.

Each deathcare practice serves different emotional, theological, and practical needs. Some people believe a body is necessary theologically and so prefer burial. Other people choose cremation, so they can keep the remains of a body nearby or spread cremains somewhere meaningful. And a lot of people don't have any idea of the possibilities, leaving their animal with the vet and later wondering, "What happened to her?"

Whatever option we choose reveals a lot about the hopes we hold about what happens after death. As an animal chaplain, I help people understand their options but always stop short of making any decision for them or judging options according to a binary of right or wrong. I also avoid privileging one practice over another for very practical reasons. For example, home burial may not be appropriate for someone who lives in a fifth-floor, walk-up studio apartment. Cremation will likely not be an option for someone passionate about the environment. Spiritual folks may want help with a funeral or memorial service. Atheists may be more comfortable with a keepsake, and so on.

While health-care proxies, living wills, and preplanning funerals have become popular for humans, people often avoid thinking about animal-companion death. But the same logic applies. By reflecting while we are sound of mind, we may make better decisions and decrease our stress at the time of death. Understanding the available options *before* a decision is necessary can help us think more clearly about how to provide our dearly beloved a sacred sendoff.

Cremation

The majority of pets are cremated by exposure to intense heat—either in a group or as individual cremation. Some people want only their animal's cremains returned and are willing to pay a higher price for this. Others are fine having their pet intermingled with others. While vase-shaped urns used to be the most common landing place for cremains, now there is an astonishing array of designs, shapes, and other options. Interestingly, in one study, people cited cremation as a way to keep an animal in the family after death.[65]

When the first cat I lived with after leaving my parent's home died, the vet asked me, "What would you like to do with him?" I was flabbergasted. I had no idea. As a kid, when cats went to the vet at the end of their life, they never returned. "You mean I can have him back?" I asked quizzically. And thus, I was educated on cremation. Mr. Kitty was a completely black, shiny cat with impeccable manners. Upon receiving his ashes back in a nondescript plastic baggie, I thought, "This will not do for classy Mr. Kitty!" A web search for "black cat urn" returned a glossy, ceramic statue of a cat, with a large, plugged hole in the bottom for inserting the ashes. It was perfect.

By the time another feline, Ringo Petricelli, succumbed to diabetes, I was well versed in urn options. Ringo's last few weeks of life were heartbreaking as his body started to fail. We were unable to get him regulated, no matter what food or insulin we tried. Soon, his eyes went dull, and he stopped walking due to pain. Unsure if it was time for euthanasia and feeling guilty, I had a frank talk with Ringo. I apologized for not being able to "fix" him and my complicity in his health problems. Then, I explained the possibility of reincarnation to the best of my ability, noting that while I was not 100 percent sure about the exact details, I thought there was a possibility he could get a new body. Each morning after this, I asked, "Ringo Petricelli, do you want a new body yet?" He would look down and walk off. Then one day, when I asked, he raised his head and stared into my eyes intensely for over a minute. Something powerful happened in that moment. It felt like shared acceptance. A few hours later, his hind end gave out, and we were off to the vet. Ringo's cremains now rest in a foot-tall Egyptian-styled urn with the head of a cat, reminiscent of the goddess Bastet. Next to him, little Max's cremains rest in a bright white Buddha figure.

While it felt most reverent for me, then, to have these felines cremated by fire individually, I soon learned the shadow side of this choice—it is not friendly to our planet. Sustaining the heat needed for cremation requires a lot of fuel and releases carbon dioxide and toxins into the air.[66] In fact, the cremation of an average-sized dog releases about 100 lbs. of greenhouse gases.[67]

Aquamation

For this reason, environmentally conscious people who still want "to keep" cremains can turn to water cremation—officially called *alkaline hydrolysis* and sometimes called *aquamation, resomation,* or *flameless cremation.* (Your vet may not be familiar with this option, so you may need to Google "aquamation near me" to research your options.) Because a hot alkaline solution does the bio-decompostion work, this process has only about a tenth of the carbon footprint of conventional cremation and releases zero emissions from the body. After processing, the "water" can be used for practical uses, such as fertilizer. Or it may simply enter the local sewer system. And the powdered bone remains will be given to you to take home.

Creative Cremains

In the last decade, the business of cremains keepsakes has exploded. You can purchase jewelry to wear ashes that comes with a tiny funnel for inserting cremains, keeping a reminder of your loved one ever present. Or buy a plushie toy animal with a zippered compartment to insert remains in. Memory boxes include a frame for displaying a photo of your animal companion on the lid. Cremains can be pressed into a vinyl record or even mixed with tattoo ink. Some people use the ashes to make cremation art—the truly talented ones fashioning a portrait of the animal.

For those who prefer Spot or Daisy to become part of nature after cremation or aquamation, I note that pet cremains can become part of an ocean reef. Or you can scatter them in a meaningful location (laws vary by state but are notoriously difficult to enforce). Bio urns use cremains to grow a tree (although a green burial could do so as well). Fido's remains can also be shot into space.

One day, my husband even received some unexpected cremains via the United States Postal Service. Like many people, he "lost his dog" via a divorce, as Amber relocated to another state with Sean's ex-wife. Upon Amber's passing, Veronica portioned out some of the ashes into a small wooden box and popped them into the mail. So, a bit of Sean's beloved dog also sits on the shelf with my dad and the felines, a stunning testament to the bonds that transcend changes in human marital status.

A quick tip if you decide to spread the love as well: When shipping cremains, use the United States Postal Service's special Label 139 or their "Cremated Remains

Animal Kit." (Most other shipping companies such as UPS, DHL, and FedEx will not knowingly accept or transport cremains.)

Home Burial

Depending on whose numbers you look at, it's estimated that somewhere between 10 percent to 25 percent of companion animals are buried. (It's hard to know precisely because some people bury cremains, which messes up percentage reporting.) The choice to bury comes with another decision, of course: *Where?* Before Sean and I got married, and I dragged him out to the country, we both lived in New York City. While my apartment lacked anywhere to bury a pet, Sean's building included a typical city patio behind it, surrounded by a bit of earthy area enclosed within a high wooden fence. So, that's where his cats ended up upon their deaths. And also a few of his brother's feline roommates, too.

Home burial is common when an animal dies at home. If you decide to bury on your property, it's a good idea to check your state and city guidelines. Also, consider how long you expect to live in the home and whether there is a location you can bury the body that is clear from any water sources, such as a well.

If you cannot bury the body immediately, make sure to store the pet somewhere cool. Be aware that fluids may pass from the body as well, so best not to lay them on your bed or other soft surfaces that might absorb anything wet. Burial should happen as quickly as possible since the body will start to decompose. (And your local laws may require a specific timeframe.) Upon burial, make sure the grave is at least a few feet deep, and avoid burying your pet in plastic. With some preplanning, you can order a pet casket online to be shipped to your home if you like. These come in both biodegradable and impenetrable styles. You can also consider a Euthabag for transporting and/or burying an animal. If the animal has had chemotherapy, be sure to select an impenetrable covering so that chemicals do not make their way into the soil or groundwater. And don't forget to check for underground power lines (just call your utility company, and they can advise).

For small animals—like hamsters, guinea pigs, or birds—or small budgets, a hand-decorated cardboard box can be transformed into a beautiful burial container. Make sure to use biodegradable decorations—and skip the glitter, which is notoriously unfriendly to the planet and can take 1,000 years to biodegrade.[68] (Also, beware, some glitters are made from insects or fish scales, thus exploit other beings.) After you complete your burial, make sure to put something heavy on top of the grave for a while—like a big pot of flowers. This has both spiritual and practical purposes. Marking the grave with something beautiful can provide a lovely place to sit and reflect. It also provides a barrier to ensure other animals don't go digging up your little buddy.

Burials for larger animals, such as horses, are more complicated. The Humane Society of the United States provides a list of state-by-state resources. In other countries, check with your local animal welfare organizations.

Sometimes when a pet dies at an animal hospital, the vet refuses to release the body for home burial. If this happens to you, ask them to provide a written reason why or show you evidence of a governmental law. Preplanning helps here, too—if home burial is important to you, make this clear to your vet while the pet is still living so that the vet understands your expectations.

And if you rent, you're probably out of luck for home burial.

Cemeteries

That's where pet cemeteries—like the ones described in the opening of this book—come in. The International Association of Pet Cemeteries & Crematories website (iaopcc.org) offers a searchable database for 15 countries. While not all pet cemeteries are associated with the organization, many are, so it is a good place to start your search.

Admittedly, some animal lovers wish to have their pets buried with them—or on the flip side, be buried with their animal companions. Most human cemeteries prohibit animal burial out of concern that it will offend other humans (and we're back to talking about *speciesism*). While it is fairly easy to slip some animal ashes into a human coffin or covertly mix them with human ashes, what options do people have if they want to be on the up-and-up? Or if they wish to feature a pet's name on a memorial marker?

Whether this is permissible depends on both state laws and individual cemetery rules. Until recently, in my state of New York, animal burial was not allowed in human cemeteries. That changed due to legislation passed in 2016. The New York Pet Burial Law enables state-regulated not-for-profit cemeteries to allow the interment of cremated remains of domestic pets with people (but notably, not on their own). It's important to point out the law does not *require* any cemetery to allow the inclusion of pet cremains. And if a human cemetery does offer animal burial, rules apply, including providing proof the cremains came from a licensed facility and a stipulation they cannot be intermingled with human cremains.[69]

Interestingly, in my state, while human cemeteries come under the purview of the Division of Cemeteries, pet cemeteries are not considered to be cemeteries but rather businesses. So, pet cemeteries are not subject to the same laws that regulate human cemeteries. This designation has impacts. On the downside, they are subject to a lot of taxes that human cemeteries are not.

On the plus side, many will gladly allow a human to be buried with an animal, space permitting. I recently spoke with Ed Martin at the Hartsdale Pet Cemetery about this. He noted that in the 40-plus years he and his family have run the cemetery, a very small percentage of people do this. And any humans must have their cremains placed within the existing pet's plot, which means people who want their full bodies to be buried are out of luck.

Due to this quandary—as well as increasing awareness of the environmental toll of cremating bodies—there's a growing movement supporting whole family cemeteries, especially those which offer green burial for any species. The Green Pet-Burial Society promotes "conservation whole family cemeteries" where interspecies family members can be buried next to or near each other in a protected wildlife preserve that supports and provides safety to other living beings. Founder Eric Greene offers, "Earth is our home; it is what we are part of. Death puts things in perspective—and at the end, there is only nature and our stewardship of this planet and life on it."[70]

Recomposition

An interesting, and somewhat related, development in deathcare practices is *recomposition*. Rather than reserving land for burial or having cremains placed symbolically near a tree trunk, recomposition advocates suggest we can use dead bodies to support and heal existing natural areas.

If you live in the Pacific Northwest, your animal companion can become part of a reforestation project. Greg Schoenbachler and Paul Tschetter's company Rooted uses an "automated system comprised of pods, each equipped with calibrated sensors that provide continuous feedback to the control system. This system deploys precise quantities of air and water tailored in real time to each pod's requirements."[71] Most of the time, animals are communally composted in the pods, and the soil is donated to partner organizations. For an additional cost, though, they can recompose a single pet and return the soil to you for your own use.

Also referred to as *earth cremation*, the process takes about eight weeks and costs about $100 for group recomposition. While some of us might balk at this idea, ecological deathcare is also a growing trend for humans. Recompose, another company in the Pacific Northwest, will turn you into soil for about $5,500.[72] The soil can be picked up or donated to Bells Mountain Conservation Forest so your remains can help leafy beings.

Taxidermy

Up until now, we've been talking about how to turn a body into something else—ash or cremains or soil. But what if you want to preserve a body?

While I am adamantly opposed to animals being killed for sport or trophy taxidermy, as a critical thinker, I have to ask: *Why does it seem okay to turn a pet into ash or soil—but not to freeze-dry him?* I suspect it has to do with our beliefs about what we deem as *natural* and *unnatural.*

Opinions on taxidermy vary widely. For example, Dr. Elliot Katz, founder of In Defense of Animals, suggested dignity should be a consideration, "If we felt [taxidermy] was a respectful thing to do, then it would be done to humans as well."[73] In contrast, animal studies scholar Christina Colvin offers, "Even when we keep in mind that pets represent 'humanized animals,' must we grieve them as we grieve humans for that grief to be valid? Or might pet taxidermy offer a possibility for grief work particular to the experience of losing a beloved companion animal?" Reviewing letters from customers to a pet taxidermy company, Colvin observed, "Taxidermy enables common forms of interaction between humans and pets such as touching, holding, and looking at to continue after the pet's death."[74]

This reflection reminds me of the comfort I feel when I pick up one of my cat's urns and say, "Hey there, little buddy. I miss you." I'll confess, I've been known to give Mr. Kitty's black cat-shaped urn a little rub from time to time. And I'll disclose that I take Beanie Babies on my book tours to talk to. (I call them "the dudes.") While this admission may cause you to suggest I have read *The Velveteen Rabbit* a few too many times, I ask you to be kind. There is something about the physicality of talking *to* something with eyes—even if they are plastic—which can be useful in tackling my loneliness.

In fact, animatronic pets are now being used to help older animal-loving adults who cannot manage the physical or financial commitments a fluffy four-legged furball requires. Older adults can be reticent to adopt a new pet, fearing what will happen to the animal upon their death. Alzheimer's and dementia can bring additional complications. And people who live in nursing homes or assisted living facilities may be prohibited from having animal companions at all. Results of a recent study revealed that adults who interacted frequently with animatronic pets indicated a decrease in loneliness plus improved mental well-being, resilience, and purpose.[75] Interestingly, some participants described using their robopets in social settings, which helped them improve their social interactions with other humans.

So, while I question the lack of consent related to taxidermy, I can understand why some people might be drawn to preserving their animal companion's bodies.

Mummification

On a somewhat related note, what about mummification for preservation? Indeed, it's possible. Seattle-based company Summum will wrap a body for inclusion in a casket or sculpt a clay form of your pet to cast a bronze or stainless-steel sarcophagus. So far, I have yet to meet anyone who has used this method, but I remain intrigued by it.

Here's how Summum describes their process: The body is bathed and cleansed. An incision is made to remove the internal organs, which are also washed. All is then immersed in a "baptismal font filled with a special preservation solution made up of certain fluids, some of which are chemicals used in genetic engineering."[76] The body and organs remain submerged for a while, then are placed back inside the body, and the incision is closed. At this point, the body is cleansed again and covered with an anointing oil plus several layers of gauze. A polymer membrane is applied next, and then a layer of fiberglass resin forms a permanent seal. The mummy is then encased within a bronze or stainless-steel sarcophagus. This sarcophagus is filled with an amber resin mixed with quartz granules. Next, the openings in the sarcophagus are welded closed, and the finished product can be interred in a cemetery.

This time-consuming and labor-intensive process results in a high price tag for this preservation method, starting at $4,000 for a cat up to $67,000 for a human. The sarcophagus and casket add additional costs. I suggested to Sean we ought to try this option for Deacon or Buba-ji under the guise of "research," but we've netted out if we had that much cash lying around, we'd rather use it for our animal advocacy efforts.

Cryopreservation

I'd be remiss not to mention that some people also choose to preserve an animal's body in the hopes that someday it can be cloned. This option is not for the small of budget either. The Cryonics Institute offers both lifetime and yearly membership options. The cost of cryopreservation will run you $1,000 for a bird, $5,800 for a cat, and $5,800+ for a dog (charged by weight). A cheaper option allows you to cryopreserve just a small tissue sample and DNA for $98. Yearly membership dues for both options currently run $120, which you'll pay every year until such time as it's scientifically possible, as well as legal, to clone your animal companion.[77]

While my sci-fi sensibilities go wild imagining cryonics, I'm not convinced that a clone of any of my companion animals' bodies would be valuable for me or them. Now, if the scientists could replicate their consciousness as well, that would be another story. I admit this dream is highly influenced by Richard Morgan's novel *Altered Carbon,* in which bodies are exchangeable, and consciousness is stored in small disks that can be placed into any body. If your "skin" (aka body) gets killed, then your "stack" (aka consciousness) can be placed in another skin. Unless your stack is destroyed, of course, in which case you are "real dead."[78]

The combination of Morgan's book and cryopreservation got me thinking about my animal companions. What might Max be like in another form? What if we could have traded his broken orange furry body for a working one? Would a cloned Max act like the original Max? While these may be dreams or thought experiments for most of us, people who believe in cryonics have faith that someday there will be answers to these questions.

When There is No Body

One morning, our cat Cocktail headed out in the backyard for his daily outside time. He never returned home.

Filled with anguish, Sean and I tried to locate him. We put up fliers and posted on Facebook's lost animal message boards. I paid a pet alert service to robocall my neighbors. Sean called vets. I called a psychic and prayed to God for clues. While we had a few leads, which led to us wandering around strangers' yards calling, "Cocktail! Cocktail! Here, kitty-kitty," we were ultimately unsuccessful.

This type of loss is unsettling and brings a whole host of different questions: *Should you mourn an animal that might still be alive? When do you "declare" a pet is officially gone? Could I have prevented this? Why, oh why, did I let him outside? Wait, what about those fantastic stories of animals who travel cross-country over many years to be reunited with their humans?* Living amongst these questions and the uncertainty of a missing pet is heartbreaking.

The grief which comes with lost pets is real. Speak with someone about your feelings and how to cope with the loss. Don't try to go it alone in this situation just because you're not sure about the animal's life status.

It has been over six years since Cocktail left. When people occasionally ask about him, I answer, "Oh, he's still out on walkabout." I picked up this term from an Australian friend who defined *walkabout* as a rite of passage to make a spiritual transition. It was the most pleasant way I could frame my unknowing.

And yet, this past year, I realized that Cocktail would be about 22 in age. So, it is likely that if he had not transitioned from this earthly plane in those first few months, he indeed would have by now. While teaching a course on animal spirituality, I suddenly felt compelled to acknowledge Cocktail, as well as the missing animals of my students or the animals from their Animal Loss Lines.

The result of our ritual was powerful—50 people calling out the names of animals of all shapes, sizes, and species. Together, we witnessed each other's pain and honored the lives of the lost. I now offer this ritual at the end of every monthly service at the Compassion Consortium, providing an opportunity for our community to witness lost, passed, vulnerable, injured, and sick animals.

Will My Animal Companion Go to Heaven?

DEPENDING ON YOUR spiritual or religious outlook, in addition to an animal companion's body, you may feel called to attend to their spirit, soul, or metaphysical qualities. Your personal beliefs will influence the route this care takes. So, it is difficult to suggest a one-size-fits-all approach to attending to spiritual matters.

Many people may choose to hold a funeral, memorial service, or another ritual for an animal. I'll note religions have different perspectives on the purpose of death services. In many religions, a funeral does not determine what happens to an animal after their bodily death. That said, it can be beneficial for bringing comfort to grieving humans. In other traditions, particularly those who believe something else happens after death, these rituals assist the being on the journey to their next stage.

Many pet cemeteries and crematoriums have a chapel where you can hold your memorial or will allow you to perform a service graveside. Animal chaplains have lots of ideas and can help you craft a meaningful memorial. Or you can DIY it with the help of friends and family.

Check out sacredsendoffs.com/memorial for a collection of resources.

Many people's ideas about what happens to animals at death may not align with their religious community or its leadership. And so, you may have existential questions you want to discuss with an animal chaplain or spiritual counselor. I caution you not to expect perfect answers on these topics from anyone—but rather look to these people for help in navigating your response to the unanswerable questions that arise from death. Because no one can prove what we ultimately want to know about death. Especially when it comes to the matter of *souls.*

I was once asked a flurry of related questions during an online talk about animals and spirituality. Instantaneously, the queries appeared one after the other in the chat box: "In your view, do animals have spirits?" "Do they have a spirit like humans?" "Do animals have any difference in their souls compared to humankind?"

I paused for a moment. Knowing nothing about the audience and always leery of providing "absolutes," I treaded forward carefully. "So, I don't know how we would know for sure," I said. "And this is exactly the same answer that I have regarding humans. What I do know is that all beings have some sort of life force. We call it by various names—including soul, spirit, consciousness, ātman, psyche, and so on. And then, at some point, that is gone from the body. So, we have a lot of questions about what happens then. And I think all of our world's traditions give us different ideas about what that might be like, and I have tried to stay open to all of them. But I don't know for sure."

I paused, took a deep breath, and made sure the audience was with me. People often expect answers from clergy. They crave certainty from us. Not confessions of "I don't know for sure." Nevertheless, I had started, and I figured I'd better see it through.

So, I continued, "I think behind the question of 'Do animals have souls?' is not a desire to know that answer in itself. Instead, what drives it is two things: First, the message we have received that having a soul is what makes a being valuable. Second, our concern that having a soul dictates what happens to a previously living being at death—and the possibility that if a being does not have a soul, it is destined for some sort of bad state. I can tell you, I think that idea is rubbish. So, while I cannot prove whether any animal—or human for that matter—has a soul, or spirit, or any other word we might use here, I do know that physics tells us energy is never destroyed, it just changes form. So, I think that's important."

I paused again. They seemed to still be with me. So, I wrapped it up.

"However, that energy changes form when animals pass—whether it's through souls or spirit, or whether it's through their metaphysical connection with us, or whether it is because of our memories, I do know that our connection to other beings, regardless of species, continues in some way." I then admitted, "So, that's probably not the perfect yes-or-no answer that you would like to hear from me, but it's what I've got."

The chat box erupted again as people swore that their animal did indeed have a soul. A few even seemed upset with me for denying certainty in the belief of souls. What

I had been unable to articulate was that just because I can't prove that we have something we call *soul* does not mean it isn't possible. I just mean it is improvable—and I wonder, does it matter? I believe all beings that have life are valuable. *How* we have life, and what happens to that life after bodily death, remains a mystery to me. And I don't treat one being different from another based on a conception of whether or not some religious authority has declared they have a soul or not—quite the opposite. Let me be clear. Whatever humans have, I believe other animals have too. Let me unpack this for you all a bit to show you how I got there.

This perceived distinction of "soul" and "body" has intrigued humankind for millennia. Every philosopher and theologian provides their own ideas and words. They speak of resurrection or transmigration or reincarnation. They debate the *hard problem of consciousness.* And, as individuals, we pick up something here, something there, combining contradictory ideas throughout our lives to create our unique belief system.

Douglas Davies, director of the Centre for Death and Life Studies at Durham University, conducts research into the life values, beliefs, and practices related to living and dying. He observes, "If we listed the beliefs held by individuals we might very well find that they form an odd collection when viewed critically, but within the context of that person's own life history and contemporary life-circumstance they find their natural home and work well." He continues, "People often accumulate their religious view of life under the influence of a wide variety of circumstances, not through formal religious education.

This can lead to apparent contradictions in what people say, since they may well never have sat down to organize their thoughts."[79]

In my case, organizing thoughts to remove contradictions is impossible. I suspect that is true for many interfaith or interspiritual folks due to the sheer number of influences and experiences we have had. You might say my beliefs are a mashup of what my Christian preacher father taught me, combined with a dozen other religions that I have studied and participated in. (Or could this hodgepodge be an attempt to reconcile truths we know at a deeper level than belief?)

For example, I recall an early lesson on souls I received from the Brahma Kumaris, a spiritual path originating in India. At the beginning of a meditation retreat, after we had all introduced ourselves, the facilitator asked, "Now, raise your hand if you have a soul." Hands shot up all over the room—*Of course, we had souls!* Gently, Sister Dorothy burst our collective bubble. "Well, no, dear ones, you do not *have* souls." Confused faces scanned other confused faces around the room. "You *are* souls," she revealed. "You are souls who think they are bodies." As she continued laying out the implications of this revelation, it all seemed to make a lot of sense. I liked the idea that souls migrated after death to new bodies. Something is comforting in that, and so I am willing to entertain it as a possibility. For the Brahma Kumaris, a soul always stays in the same species from life to life. A human will always return human; a cat will always be a cat. (And so, you see why I offered Ringo Petricelli the promise of a new body.)

Of course, I also find the Buddhist philosophy I learned in dharma training compelling, especially the suggestion that for seven weeks after death in the *bardo* (or between) state, an animal may still have some awareness of me, even though we are no longer together physically. And so, during this time, Buddhists suggest we should continue to speak to the animal, offer prayers, and recite mantras for them to assist in their next rebirth, which may or may not be birthed as the same species. (And so, this is why I believe little ginger Max is now the bright-orange squirrel playing walnut kickball in our attic.)

Even though I fiercely debated my seminary professors about Christian views regarding death, amusingly, I think that when my father's cat, Sam, died, he was reunited with Dad in some other realm, and they now hang out together. I realize that this contradicts what I've already offered about Max and Ringo. My belief about Sam is fueled by a single sermon on animal death that I discovered in the over 1,500 sermons I inherited when my father died. In it, he recants the story of a young child in his congregation asking, "Will my dog go to Heaven?" Then he notes, "Little did the young girl know the depth of the simple question which she had asked. Even less did she know to what extent her teacher would research her question because he too, as a child, had wondered about his own dog."

The remainder of the sermon chronicles my father's research. Returning to the Sunday school class the next weekend, he delivered his answer: "You know, I think they do because Heaven is when we feel God very near. Heaven is when we feel happy, safe, friendly, and loved. Sometimes we feel that way right now. But sometimes, something comes along, and we feel sad and hurt. Heaven is a place where that will never happen, and it might be a long way off. God's happiness never ends, even though we might die and leave our family, friends, and pets. But sometimes they leave us first, like your dog. I think God has a special place for our pets because they are very special to us. Does that help you in your sadness?"[80]

Although my theological outlook about God and my father's outlook are not identical, nor was our seminary training similar—his, 20th-century Christian; mine, 21st-century Interspiritual—we approach the question of animal souls with one crucial commonality: Animals matter from a sacred perspective.

Working with people from different traditions makes my language about this fluid, as I use different sacred words depending on that person's spiritual context. Yet, regardless of this diversity of concepts of *What's Next?*, here is where I ultimately net out: Whatever human animals "have," other animals do too.

As to what that means for an afterlife, you would think that graduating from a couple of seminaries and studying myriad religious traditions, I would know for sure. But I'm back to two words I often utter, "It depends." And, in this case, I mean, it depends on whom you ask.

So, one might ask, then, "What good is clergy?"

My conviction is that rather than provide answers, chaplains help people navigate their questions themselves and handle the emotions that arise from unanswerable queries.

We help people learn to embrace unknowing.

In this regard, I find incredibly helpful the words of poet Charles Bukowski, who once proclaimed, "Animals never worry about Heaven or Hell. Neither do I. Maybe that's why we get along."[81] Amen, Mr. Bukowski. And so, instead of going in circles in theoretical or theological conversations, we can:

- Acknowledge the loss and provide our animal companions a sacred sendoff that honors their life and our relationship with them.
- Get the support we need for processing our grief—not hide it, suppress it, apologize for it, or wish it would go away. Instead, we can recognize the grief is a result of deep love. And once we give that love somewhere to go again, we will feel better and become regrounded in our lives.
- Strengthen our continuing bonds with our animal companions through talking to them, as well as through meditation, prayer, and remembrance.

No, readers, our animal companions have not vanished. They have been transformed. Our enduring connections with them remain for the rest of our lives. And, hopefully, even beyond that.

Chapter 7

EXPANDING CREATURELY COMPASSION

*I*N THE SUMMER of 1983, my family spent a week at Ghost Ranch Education & Retreat Center in Abiquiú, New Mexico. I can pinpoint the year because *Star Wars: Return of the Jedi* was playing in theaters, and I vividly remember being resentful about missing it. I also recall my father was teaching a workshop on C. S. Lewis. As avid fans of *The Lion, the Witch and the Wardrobe* book series, my sister and I were disappointed to find out that Dad's class topic was not Aslan, but rather some bible stuff written from the Book of Luke.

"Luke *Skywalker*?" I asked. Did my dad mean that sometimes courageous, yet often whiny protagonist of the first *Star Wars* film who braved danger and failure to destroy Darth Vader's evil Death Star weapon and save the Galaxy?! "Nope, not that Luke," my father conceded.

His lessons were obviously not targeted to kids, so my sister and I were promptly signed up for a chaperoned overnight hiking trip. Just moments into the trek,

I found a flat frog splayed wide on the dirt road, all four legs pointing in different directions. I could not leave him there. Yet, I wasn't carrying my own pack, and my pockets weren't big enough. So, I tied a string to one leg, and I dragged him along until I could find the right burial location.

I remember, but not precisely why, that I did not dispose of my new buddy that night. Upon our return to the retreat center the following day, my mother informed me that the frog was *not* to enter our room and suggested that perhaps I should return it to the road where I found it. So I buried the frog under a nearby tree.

Amusingly, over dinner that night, my father mentioned that earlier that day he had lectured on the biblical parable referred to as the Good Samaritan. The synchronicity of this was perfect. Let me explain.

The Parable of the Good Samaritan

IN THIS STORY, which appears in the Gospel attributed to Luke, a rebellious new Jewish teacher named Jesus has just been asked a question: "Teacher, what shall I do to inherit eternal life?" Jesus asks the questioner if he knows what the ethical guidelines of their shared faith said on the matter. (Because Jesus and his followers were Jewish. "Christianity" and "Christians" do not develop as a separate religion or identity until well after Jesus's death.) The inquirer proves he knows the rules by stating, "You shall love the Lord your God with all your heart, and with all your soul, and with all your strength, and with all your mind; and your neighbor as yourself" (Luke 10:27, New

Revised Standard Version). Jesus replies this answer was correct. And that should be the end of the story.

But it is not, because the man has a specific motive in asking the question. He wants Jesus to divulge who exactly he has to love as himself. He scrutinizes, "And who is my neighbor?" At this critical point, Jesus doesn't answer the question directly, but rather through a teaching story. He offers this:

> A man was going down from Jerusalem to Jericho and fell into the hands of robbers, who stripped him, beat him, and went away, leaving him half dead. Now, by chance, a priest was going down that road; and when he saw him, he passed by on the other side. So, likewise, a Levite, when he came to the place and saw him, passed by on the other side. But a Samaritan while traveling came near him; and when he saw him, he was moved with pity. He went to him and bandaged his wounds, having poured oil and wine on them. Then he put him on his own animal, brought him to an inn, and took care of him. The next day he took out two denarii, gave them to the innkeeper, and said, 'Take care of him; and when I come back, I will repay you whatever more you spend' (Luke 10:31–35).

After telling this story, Jesus asks, "Which of these three, do you think, was a neighbor to the man who fell into the hands of the robbers?" The original questioner— apparently having lost his arrogance and perhaps feeling a little embarrassed—replies, "The one who showed him mercy." Thus, the moral is stated: The compassionate neighbor is the one who shows mercy to those judged as others. Jesus then directs the questioner to follow that example.

As I read this parable, Jesus intended the circle of in-ness to be as comprehensive as possible.[82] I root my observation on a statement found earlier in the Gospel, where Jesus states the purpose of his movement is "to proclaim release to the captives and recovery of sight to the blind, to let the oppressed go free" (Luke 4:18). Most English translations don't say captive *adults* or blind *men* or oppressed *humans.* Indeed, no gender, race, nor species is present in Jesus's mission statement.

Plus, there are plenty of other stories in the bible where Jesus shows concern for other-than-humans. In John 2:13–16, he rails against those selling captive animals to be killed, freeing the oxen, sheep, and doves.[83] In Luke 14:5, he states a moral imperative to break the Sabbath to help an animal in distress (implying that our moral duty to animals supersedes our religious obligations). And in Matthew 9:13 and 12:7, he condemns animal sacrifice.

I share these verses not because I think Christian scripture should drive everyone's ethics and actions but because they explain why—as a preacher's kid—I wondered: *What would Jesus do about injured animals on the road?* The answer seemed clear to me: If someone was hurt by the side of the road, then Jesus would want me to help them—even if they were a flattened frog.

Beyond Jesus: Animal Ethics in Other Spiritual Traditions

FOR THOSE WHO believe basing ethical considerations upon the framework of a Christian parable is problematic, no worries. The study of spiritual traditions reveals similar imperatives, often referred to generally as the Golden Rule. (Traditionally, the Golden Rule refers to the form, "Do unto others as you would have them do unto you." When the language flips to "Do *not* do unto others as you would not have them do unto you," it is referred to as the Silver Rule. The Platinum Rule reads, "Treat others as they wish to be treated.")

The Golden Rule

Baha'i Faith *(Baha'u'llah Gleanings)*	Lay not on any soul a load that you would not wish to be laid upon you, and desire not for anyone the things you would not desire for yourself.
Buddhism *(The Buddha Udana-Varga 5:18)*	Treat not others in ways that you yourself would find hurtful.
Taoism *(Lao Tzu, T'ai Shang Kan Ying P'ein, 213–218)*	Regard your neighbor's gain as your own gain, and your neighbor's loss as your own loss.
Christianity *(Jesus, Matthew 7:12)*	In everything, do to others as you would have them do to you; for this is the law.

Islam (The Prophet Muhammad, Hadith)	Not one of you truly believes until you wish for others what you wish for yourself.
Native Spirituality (Chief Dan George)	We are as much alive as we keep the Earth alive.
Jainism (Mahavira, Sutrakritanga)	One should treat all creatures in the world as one would like to be treated.
Hinduism (Mahabharata 5:1517)	This is the sum of duty: do not do to others what would cause pain if done to you.
Confucianism (Confucius Analects 15.23)	One word which sums up the basis of all good conduct… loving-kindness. Do not do to others what you do not want done to yourself.
Judaism (Hillel, Talmud, Shabbat 31a)	What is hateful to you, do not do to your neighbor. This is the whole Torah; all the rest is commentary.
Sikhism (Guru Granth Sahib, 1299)	I am a stranger to no one; and no one is a stranger to me. Indeed, I am a friend to all.
Zoroastrianism (Shayast-na-Shayast 13.29)	Do not do unto others whatever is injurious to yourself.
Unitarianism (Unitarian principle)	We affirm and promote respect for the interdependent web of all existence of which we are a part.

Source.— Pflaum Publishing Group. *The Golden Rule Poster*. Table/Poster #5003. n.d. Dayton, OH. pflaum.com/preview/goldrule/goldrule.pdf.

Granted, how these ideals are actualized in individual adherent's actions varies widely. Still, it is remarkable that across the spectrum of spiritual traditions, we find people trying to answer the same question: *How should I treat others?*

Animals Doing unto Each Other

BEFORE MOVING ON, it is essential to note that humans are not the only species to exhibit concern beyond their own wellbeing. There is an increasing body of work in studying the *prosociality* of various species who behave in ways that benefit others. Studies have revealed that many animals share resources such as space and food, cooperate in gathering food or solving problems, and behave altruistically.[84] Helping behavior has been seen in dolphins, gulls, apes, bats, and bonobos, among others.[85] Interestingly, animals imprisoned in human systems comfort or assist each other too. For example, in one study of dairy cows, "social licking and gentle head rubbing were higher between dairy cows after they experienced negative human contacts in the milking parlor."[86] Similarly, uncaged rats intentionally freed caged rats, even forgoing nearby chocolate to do so—and then went on to get the chocolate and share it with the liberated.[87]

Although a deep dive into other-than-human animal behavior is out of scope for this book, the acknowledgment that animals act out of concern for each other is vital for dismantling the idea that humans are solely responsible for the "stewardship" of other species. Paradoxically, animals may support each other to recover from the stress and trauma of their interactions with "caretaking" humans.

Dealing with Dilemmas

OF COURSE, BACK in 1983 in New Mexico, my exegetical and interfaith research skills were not nearly as honed as they are today. Instead, I rooted my argument for interspecies compassion more in *Star Wars* than in the Book of Luke: It doesn't matter what species you are; the Rebel Alliance will take care of you. Whether you are a short green Jedi Master with big ears, an android, a Wookie, a human, or a frog—you are valuable. As an adult, I can now shoot plentiful laser shots through my childhood apologetics. The Rebel Alliance did not value all lives, killing their share of Imperial Stormtroopers. Yet, my belief in the possibility of galaxy-wide interspecies inclusivity affected me deeply.

While some people might write off this admission as the musings of an overly excited fangirl or budding transhumanist ethicist, I caution you not to. The impact of modern narratives and pop culture in forming our beliefs about who deserves compassion should not be understated. From *Star Wars* to *Star Trek, E.T., Alien, Men in Black*, and countless other stories, we explore—and confess—the challenges of living with other species.

While the animal neighbors we come across every day may not be as fantastical as those in our galactic imaginations, it's clear that we wrestle with how to treat other beings even outside of religious traditions. Perhaps the most important thing we can do as animal lovers is to get really curious about the challenges facing other creatures and how inspired people are making a difference in these animals' lives and deaths.

In the next chapter, we'll consider the free-living beings outside our homes yet on the fringes of our view—the ones who dart under our decks and fill the trees over our roofs.

Then we'll move on to the beings who roam grassy savannas in Africa, climb treacherous mountains in the US National Parks, and who are transported far from home by humans. Next, we'll consider the challenges faced by farmed animals, ocean dwellers, animal astronauts, and beings claimed by corporations. Along the way, we'll learn some surprising facts about these animals with the hope of expanding our creaturely compassion in their direction. And, of course, we'll consider how to give them sacred sendoffs.

Chapter 8

FREE-LIVING, WILD BEINGS

*D*URING MY TEENS in Michigan, I was lectured by hunting neighbors about why deer populations needed to be culled and how guns could help. I didn't buy it. Amy and I spent most Sunday nights watching Mutual of Omaha's *Wild Kingdom*, so I had a firm belief that nature could simply take care of itself. Plus, there was all the expertise I had gleaned from the Junior Ranger programs we were enrolled in on summer vacations.

I vividly recall one such trip to Grand Teton National Park. I must have been about nine, and my mother had just informed us that *téton* was French for *nipple*. Amy and I spent much of the vacation cracking jokes and spelling out BOOB—or more precisely 8008—on our pocket calculators. (Why we were traveling with calculators, I have no idea. I like to think we were early tech adopters.)

With embarrassment, I also remember what I refer to as *the public humiliation*, and what my mother refers to as *why I had to throw away Sarah's blue hoodie*. On the day of this event, my sister and I took a wilderness hike with a park ranger. This courageous fellow had been assigned to a group of rambunctious kids so that parents could have a break. Ranger Ted gave us one task for the adventure: Find something interesting and put it in your pocket. The best "find" would win a prize. (Apparently, these were the days before the National Park Service prohibited taking stuff from parks, or else Ted was out of compliance.)

In hindsight, the plan was brilliant from a kid-management perspective. We were so busy looking at everything that we didn't have time to needle each other. With intense focus, I chose my special item and put it in the pocket of my sweatshirt. It looked like a shiny black olive but with no hole or pit. It gleamed in the sun and was smooth to the touch. I thought it might be a berry of some sort but wasn't sure. I hoped so because I was getting hungry.

When we returned to the lodge, one by one, each kid revealed their secret treasure. Reaching for mine, I was discouraged to find it had all but disintegrated. As I salvaged what I could of the crumbly mess in my pocket, an enormous grin appeared on Ranger Ted's face. "Well, my dear, that's deer poop!" he exclaimed. My fellow wee trekkers erupted in laughter, and my lip began to tremble.

That moment stands out as one where an adult unknowingly crushed my career aspirations. That's probably just as well, as it's unlikely I would have been able to handle some of the practices required for the job. Ecosystems are unfathomably complex, and ethical decisions are often as clear as mud to me.

Who Lives on the Planet?

WOULD IT SURPRISE you to hear that less than 4 percent of mammals and 30 percent of the world's birds are "wild"? And yet, according to the 2018 report *Biomass Distribution on Earth,* that's the case. Thanks to humans, our planet—once thriving with biodiversity of feathered, finned, scaled, furry, and leafy varieties—is now primarily used for supporting livestock. What's more, in the process of using more and more land for human purposes, human beings have caused the loss of 83 percent of all wild mammals since the dawn of civilization.[88]

Feeding this problem (pun intended) is our cultivation of over one-third of the Earth's landmass for grazing and growing crops to feed farmed animals. Indeed, animal agriculture has led to the destruction of almost 91 percent of the Amazon rainforest, home to 2,000 species of animals, including 427 mammal species, 1,300 bird species, 378 species of reptiles, and more than 400 species of amphibians![89] Beyond the deaths of the individual animals and entire species extinction, this loss of habitat could be considered another death.

Let's Face It, We Don't Always Share Well

EVEN THE LAND we supposedly have left wild is altered by human actions. Environmental archaeologist Terry O'Connor explains, "We are making small but significant changes to the composition of the atmosphere, major changes to the ecology of all but the deepest oceans, and we have radically altered the composition and distribution of plant and animal communities all across the Earth's land surfaces."[90]

Of course, environmental modification isn't uniquely human. Most species alter their environments. O'Connor points to the mounds termites and ants create or how marine invertebrates create coral reefs. Then he goes even further, acknowledging the changes made by green plants "which have permanently altered the Earth's atmosphere by dumping into it their metabolic waste product, that highly reactive and dangerous gas oxygen."[91] Admittedly, we don't typically view plants that way, do we? Instead, we presume they are placed here *for* us; their job being to make the air breathable.

Just because other species are involved in altering Earth, it doesn't let us off the hook, though—as humanity is by far the most significant modifier of the planet. We cause disturbances when we engage in long-term actions such as creating buildings and roads. Furthermore, we make short-term disruptions: any time we clear refuse, mow lawns, and prune parks, each one of us has the potential to impact other species. We also love to redirect and concentrate surface water, determining what should stay dry and where it is okay to have wetness. As O'Connor observes, "Those water bodies are then usually managed to ensure that only a limited, tolerated range of other species makes use of them: ducks are allowed, leeches are not."[92]

We replace what we consider undesirable with what we deem desirable: planting flower beds and vegetable gardens and removing what we categorize as weeds or consider inappropriate for our yards. We also affect the animals around us. For example, there's what my husband

Sean did to the carpenter ants in our pantry last week and also the mourning doves, goldfinches, and starlings he has attracted with bird feeders. Of course, I'm also letting the eastern gray squirrels eat the birdseed he purchases (if the red-bellied woodpeckers don't get to it first). And each spring, I yell at the mama red-tailed hawk not to eat "my" chipmunks while I try to provide them with plenty of places to hide.

Humans also tend to deposit a lot of refuse. While we may be tempted to think, *I do not litter!,* we need to take a closer look. In addition to our composted food scraps or recycled Amazon delivery boxes, we must consider our bodily waste, discarded things, problematic plastic, and the seemingly endless byproducts that must be discarded after our "stuff" is created.

Finally, we create routeways and communications infrastructures: poles, lines, towers, and jets disturb the sky while roads, rails, and subway tunnels traverse the ground. These can create *zones of enhanced mortality.*[93]

All these modifications create greater risks for the beings with whom we share our geographical locales—as we preference human needs over those of others. And yet, it's not all bad news. Through these actions, humans also create opportunities for other species. Consider the habitat of a garbage dump, rich in nutrients and a potential energy source for some critters or the green corridors of our road systems that provide routeways for small mammals like possums and woodchucks; even our skyscrapers are habitats for urban birds. For millennia, many wild species have been closely associated with us yet are not technically under human management.

These "free" animals are impacted by humans and yet

maintain a certain amount of autonomy. Of course, it's important to point out that free animals are not determined by species but rather by their individual ecological locations. For example, a rabbit could be free within a field. On the flip side, if caged in a lab, the rabbit is being commercially exploited.

Some species are considered *commensal* or *synanthropic* (literally "with people"). This means they use human habitations for living space and food. The well-fed chipmunks and mice living in my backyard would fit this category. They are free-living, and yet their populations would be much less viable (or their lifestyles significantly changed) if not for the environment my husband and I create. Their lifeways are connected with ours. And so, it should not be surprising that their death ways are as well.

Sometimes we are aware of these connections and other times oblivious. I've already mentioned two in this chapter: macro-level species extinctions and microlevel deaths in my pantry. Now consider this event in India: Soon after the drug Diclofenac was introduced in the 1990s to relieve pain in cows, the vulture population was decimated—by over 97 percent![94] What happened? When the cattle died, vultures fed on them and ingested the drug. Unfortunately, Diclofenac turned out to be toxic for birds. Eventually, the Indian government banned the drug. Still, the impact was substantial: Zoroastrians dispose of human bodies after death by leaving them in elevated Towers of Silence, open to the elements, so that vultures may strip the bones clean. Dead vultures meant the human dead also had a problem.

This type of problem isn't limited to India, of course.

Innumerable animals die worldwide due to human actions gone astray. And animals also perish naturally, of course.

How We Respond to Wild Losses

WHILE RESEARCH ON how humans respond to companion animal loss is widely available, insights about responses to other animal losses are more anecdotal. Let's look at one example.

In October 2017, distraught hikers filed a report with the California Department of Fish and Wildlife (CDFW) after coming across a group of more than 74 dead and dying mule deer in the Inyo National Forest. Additional reports followed.[95] The CDFW investigated the incident and released their findings, citing treacherous ice on the deer's migration route led to slippery conditions, causing the animals to lose footing, plunging hundreds of feet onto the sharp boulders below. Soon, a heated social media debate commenced about what *should* have been done, criticizing the CDFW's no interference policy.

"Folks were pretty traumatized by these dead deer," Tom Stephenson, senior environmental scientist for the department, reported to *Outdoor California*. "People may think the deaths represent a devastating event for some Eastern Sierra deer populations. It is not." The interviewer, seeking perhaps to console her readers, assured them, "These naturally occurring deaths, although shocking, do not significantly impact the deer population and pose no threat to human life."[96] Well, it may not be devastating for the population as a whole, but few could deny it was devastating for those individual deer. And while the incident may not have posed a threat to human life, the quotes above seem to deny the right to grieve other-than-human losses.

In spiritual or religious contexts, we praise Creation or the interconnected web of life yet can be remarkably unaware of the day-to-day experiences of the beings we are supposedly connected to. I often hear remarks about how nature will always restore itself to balance. There's a bypass of sorts: *Not my problem. I don't want to know.*

But where does that leave us when we hear about geese rounded up to be gassed because people don't like their presence in parks? Or swans that are killed so that jetski-ers and boaters can use waterways where they nest? Or wild horses and burros being slaughtered so that ranchers can exploit public lands? These aren't problems of nature. These are anthrozooloogical issues, constantly happening all around us.

Preventing the Losses We Can

WHAT IS OUR responsibility to the other beings with whom we share the planet? Should we get involved when free-living wild beings are in trouble? It can seem overwhelming to decide where to even start. Luckily, animal protection organizations that are well versed in these quandaries provide easy tools that can help you get involved from your living room. For example, In Defense of Animals (IDA) offers a robust program that helps both animals and the humans who support them. Each morning with my tea, I jump on their website (idausa.org/

take-action/) and check out who I can help with the click of a button. IDA's platform then sends out personalized letters to decision-makers and suggests other actions I can do to help, such as phone scripts and social media sample text to use for that specific initiative, plus they keep you updated on how the initiative goes and what impact it has.

Lisa Levinson, head of IDA's Wild Animals Campaign, reflecting on balancing the needs of humans and animals by considering environmental factors, told me, "Animals especially depend on their surroundings for survival. When development reduces prime habitat for wild animals, they lose access to survival resources like food, water, and shelter. Without survival resources, animals may forage or hunt closer to human communities, increasing human-animal conflicts. For example, coyotes may hunt in suburban neighborhoods and geese may nest in office complexes or public parks. Until our society embraces the importance of coexistence with our animal neighbors, conflicts will continue to result in animal suffering, such as coyote killing contests and lethal goose roundups."[97]

Beyond advocating for animals in trouble, we can also become mindful of the ways we cross paths with other wildlife on a day-to-day basis. For example, we can make sure our homes don't have hazards, such as window wells that animals can fall into or toxic weed killers in our yards. Here's an easy, lifesaving hack: Avoid mowing from the outside in, since starting at the center and moving outward allows time for frogs and chipmunks to get to the outer edges and out of the way of slicing blades! At night, we can turn off the outside house lights, so insects don't fly themselves to death circling bulbs. When you view where you live as an interspecies habitat rather than "my house," each decision can become an exercise in compassion.

By far, the most problematic incidents take place while we are driving. Unquestionably, roads are far more deadly to animals than to humans. In 2020, 38,680 humans died in traffic accidents, according to the National Highway Traffic Safety Administration.[98] That's about 100 a day. Which is heartbreaking in itself. Now consider this additional statistic. It's estimated that human motorists in the US alone kill nearly 400 million animals each year. That's over a million a day.[99] And so, I think we must acknowledge our part in what is going on and consider whether there are some actions we might be willing to take as a result of this data.

Driving slowly and without distractions helps. So does learning about the animals in your locale, so you learn what to beware of when in your car. A few notable insights for my eco-location in the Northeast include watching out for toads and frogs in the spring, as breeding produces a flurry of activity. In the summer I keep an eye out for wobbly birds—since young, naïve creatures are just learning to fly—and likewise, for baby mammals who are just learning to explore on their own and have limited experience with the dangers of roads. When the nights turn cooler in the fall, I keep my eyes out for reptiles, who enjoy hanging out on warm roadbeds. And in the snowy winter, my attention turns to birds who look for sand, salt, and grain along roadsides. And of course, all year round I watch diligently for deer.[100]

And then there's the road-as-restaurant issue. Retired biology professor Roger M. Knutson, author of *Flattened*

Fauna: A Field Guide to Common Animals of Roads, Streets, and Highways, offers, "Plant food on the road (all imported) consists of seeds blown from passing grain transports, occasional bits of badly wilted lettuce from a discarded McDonald's carton, or a few potato chips from a littering child."[101] This has some implications for animals. Items tossed out of car windows or left after garbage pickup, even if organic, can create danger for animals as they nibble along routes traveled by cars. So, avoid tossing apple cores or banana peels out the window on your commute thinking, *Someone will eat them.*

Sending Off Wildlife

SADLY, WE CAN'T prevent all losses. So, how should we respond to animal deaths beyond those in our direct care? As I mentioned earlier, I have a passion for taking HBC animals to the vet and getting road-killed animals off the road to bless them. As I got serious about caring for these dead, of course, governmental laws came into play.

In the state of New York, where I live, wildlife health comes under the purview of the Department of Environmental Conservation. Yet, the removal of animals from roads falls under local, county, and state departments of transportation, based on which has oversight for the specific roadway. And most of these organizations will only deal with large animals, such as deer.

In remote locations near me, wildlife is usually pulled off the roadway into the woods to decompose naturally. Yet, in urban areas, deer bodies can attract other animals and lead to new problems, so the carcasses are moved.

While my town's DOT refused my request for an interview, the officials of a neighboring county estimate that they deal with over 1,000 dead deer each year, and so they hire a contractor, who is paid about $75 for each call. The bodies are buried in pits, taken to landfills, rendered into feed for domestic animals, or composted under massive piles of woodchips. After a few months, the compost is used to support the health of vegetation along roadways.

Some animal control officers will pick up small wildlife and incinerate their bodies. But for the most part, squirrels, raccoons, opossums, turtles, skunks, groundhogs, and other critters will receive free sky burial courtesy of our local turkey vultures and ravens. Or they might be consumed by mammals, such as the local northern flying squirrels, raccoons, and skunks. And sometimes—perhaps surprisingly—roadkill animals will be eaten by humans.

In some states, including Montana, Washington, and Missouri, it is legally permissible for people to take larger animals (such as deer and elk) which have been killed by cars home to eat—as long as they obtain a permit and adhere to other local laws.[102] A troubling side to this seemingly utilitarian concept is a concern that people may intentionally lure wildlife to road edges in order to hit them.[103] In some places, large road-killed animals can also end up rendered into food for zoos[104] or companion animals.[105]

When I started removing wildlife from the roads, biosafety was a concern. Rabies, transmissible spongiform encephalopathy, and zoonotic diseases are real. So, I have done my research and abide by the US Department of Agriculture's (USDA) Wildlife Carcass Disposal guidelines—except that I refuse to use the word *disposal.* Instead,

I refer to my action as a sacred sendoff, gently moving the body to the side of the road using heavy gloves and a sturdy shovel, careful to choose a location that will minimize the danger for other animals who may later come to the site. The flashing orange safety lights on the side of my Jeep and my strategically placed emergency warning triangles help keep me safe, as does my snazzy, neon-yellow, hi-vis vest.

Reverently, I offer a short apology on behalf of humanity for our encroachment on wildlands and our desire to drive at speeds that are hazardous to other life-forms, ending my words with "May you have a most auspicious next lifetime." If there are fallen leaves nearby, I may cover the little injured body.

When animals die around our house—for example, when Buba-ji defies me and offs a deer mouse, or a hawk drops a mangled squirrel on my deck—I place the deceased in an area I call The Vortex. It's really just a bunch of fallen tree limbs Sean stacked into a triangular structure, with a wide opening in the front sporting a flag that states "Peace to All Beings." Gently placing a tiny body inside, I cover it with foliage, profess my sadness that their life here is over, and wish them an auspicious next lifetime.

Sometimes, that's that. Other times, I return to check in. My mother reports that I was ever curious during my childhood chipmunk burials, digging their bodies up, then reburying them. She chalked this up to scientific curiosity. But, in hindsight, I think there was a spiritual component all along.

I can't explain why precisely, but I suspect it has something to do with an internalized belief in "paying my respects." As if, somehow, this being will know by my visit that their life mattered. Of course, I understand that they don't need my blessing to have a meaningful life—I'm not that arrogant. It's more an extra: *I see you, bitty mouse. In case you didn't know, you matter. Thank you for being part of this interspecies world I live in.*

At some point, I began photographing them.

I struggled with this decision. Was it okay to post images of beings without their permission? I still am not confident about the answer, but I decided yes, as long as I covered their wounds and positioned them reverently. Stumbling upon the hashtag #animalmemorial, I found other people doing the same, including Joy Muller, a self-taught taxidermist who creates stunning dioramas and taxidermy art. Rather than burying animal bodies under leaves, she preserves them.

Preserving Animal Bodies

Dragged to museums full of dusty, awkwardly posed American black bears, mink, and bison during my childhood, I've long been unresolved about taxidermy, as I noted in Chapter 6. The practice seemed to imply human dominance and filled me with discomfort. Of course, wax museums also make me uneasy, so I wonder if the problem is based on seeing something that should be alive being so still and stuck in one position. Preserving animal bodies raises a slew of questions to ponder. Do we have the right to display a being's body without their permission? Does it somehow matter why we are preserving the body?

My response to animal memorial taxidermy began a messy inquiry around these questions. First, I noticed that what I most appreciated about Joy's pieces was that they included found animals—not ones that had been hunted. For some reason, this implied a more profound reverence toward the life of the animal to me. Trophy animals say more about the achievement of the hunter than the life of the hunted. (Though an avid hunter might debate this point with me.)

Second, I was drawn to the peacefulness of the animals who seemed to embody an ideal of *the beautiful death*. (Whereas educationally displayed "specimens" tend to be positioned in awkward action poses and severed-head trophy animals often have an odd *staring off into the distance* vibe.) Third, there was a thoughtfulness to the way she delicately combined the bodies with other natural elements. Of course, I had no idea whether what I felt correlated to the artist's process or intentions. So, I reached out to learn more. Muller offered, "When I find or receive a passed animal, I treat the body like a precious and sacred gift. I find it a privilege to be given the chance to study and appreciate the amazing beauty and perfection of their form, their fur, or feathers in a way that isn't possible when they are living. I am able to preserve this beauty and perhaps in a way 'revive' them, even if it is only a re-creation of how they were in a moment captured in time."[106]

Joy acknowledged that many people don't like taxidermy or find it morbid and macabre, and yet added, "I think even if people don't like taxidermy per se, they appreciate my good intention of creating something beautiful. They feel the same way I do about these animals. They are special, treasured, and loved. The emotional connection to the animal is immediately felt."

This last answer provided some clarity about my response to her work. I did feel deeply connected to the animals I saw on her Instagram feed. I kept returning to them over and over. Although I had never met any of these creatures, in some way, to witness them felt like an act of reverence. *Don't turn away from me. See me. Acknowledge the value of my life.* Writing this book, I have felt moments of bottomless sadness. Seeing the care with which Joy treats these beings opened my heart up wide. Somewhere across the globe lives a stranger who, like me, refuses to turn away from the bodies of dead animals. At the same time, her work led me into deeper inquiry about the ethics regarding animal bodies, once deceased.

In "Freeze-Drying Fido: The Uncanny Aesthetics of Modern Taxidermy," Dr. Christina Colvin explores taxidermy, species endangerment, and extinction, curious about how animals become *grievable*. She offers, "Instead of representing humans dominating animals, performances of modern taxidermy show humans with animals, engaged in the taxidermic process as a way to work through and even critique several of the paradigms through which humans typically engage with animals. Rather than forget or efface the lives of animals, then, modern taxidermy can facilitate the work of memory by emphasizing an animal's death and the particularity of the animal who died. Furthermore, by revealing the particular rather than the representative animal, taxidermy has the potential to establish animals as subjects of grief."[107]

Checking out our response to taxidermy may be one of the best doorways of inquiry into our beliefs about "ownership" and consent regarding bodies of any species. Beyond full taxidermy, what about the use of body parts? At spiritual gatherings, I see people using bird feathers to fan the flames of a burning sage stick and placing butterflies on Ostara altars. Some traditions incorporate feathers or bones into sacred ceremonial wear. It occurs to me that animal-body preservation doesn't always mean an entire corpse.

What are the ethics of these uses? Admittedly, there may be a difference between picking up a feather dropped on the ground by a passing hawk and purchasing one from a retail shop. The latter often means the feather has been plucked painfully from a live being who is being exploited in captivity—no matter how spiritual looking the marketing might try to convince us otherwise.

We also must be cautious about appropriating cultural narratives of others to justify modern purchases. I often rub up against this issue with the instruments used in drum circles, where paradoxically, people tell me they revere the sacredness of life as they beat on another being's skin—one who was raised and killed specifically to create the instrument using methods very different than what they imagine from the "American Indian" stories they were raised with.

Likewise, some religious traditions still engage in animal sacrifice. While I am all for people's right to practice their spiritual tradition, I firmly believe these rituals need to be critically explored when they include violence towards others. Often, when we dig in to our own histories, we may need to acknowledge that our ancestors did not know about the capacity for pain and grief and spiritual connection in other species. With the awareness we have now, we can then update these rituals to retain the underlying meaning of sacrifice on a more metaphorical level while using nonviolent actions that are more compassionate.

Each time we consider taking something from an animal or doing something with an animal body, it offers us an opportunity to reflect on the intent of our action and its consequences for that being. If we dig courageously enough, we may realize what we believe is a romanticization calling for a reality check.

Natural Burials and Human Interventions

For example, in the disastrous year 2020, I watched, mortified, as animals succumbed to unprecedented wildfires in Australia and along the US West Coast. I reflected on these "natural" cremations and how the ash from their bodies would become part of the land on which they died. And then I wondered, is that true? Or am I involved in some romanticizing here?

Indeed, I was. Most animals who perish during wildfires—whether by deadly smoke inhalation, severe burns, suffocation underground, or injury—do not end up as fine ashes with bits of small bone, like the cat cremains inurned on my shelf. Instead, their bodies become subject to the natural cycle that resumes after a fire is out—or even as it sizzles—as other animals take advantage of the ground-based buffet.

Whether during a wildfire or on a typical day, how animal bodies are handled on government-managed land is determined by land managers, state laws, and federal administrative policies. Most bodies are left in place for the natural cycle of death and scavenging to progress.

Yet, park management will intervene when a body is near a designated visitor use area, campsite, or hiking trail—since large mammal carcasses can attract bears, wolves, and others who can then cause danger for humans. So, these bodies may be moved to different locations within a park or deposited in a local landfill. Perhaps the strangest sounding removal method is the use of explosives, for which detailed directions are included in the National Park Service's (NPS) "Specialized Blasting Techniques" manual.[108] Although, gruesome to consider, explosives are often more practical than cutting up and hauling out a half-ton animal many miles along a forest trail.

In disaster situations, a local government usually decides what happens, taking into account state regulations, federal laws, and Environmental Protection Agency (EPA) requirements. In general, small bodies are buried and large ones incinerated. In the event of an animal disease outbreak, the USDA's National Center for Animal Health Emergency Management kicks in, offering options for disposing of animal bodies, including composting, rendering, burial, and incineration. It even provides a fascinating, if not morbid, Carcass Management Dashboard for help to determine options and costs for "disposing" of "contaminated" animals.[109] (I note here the language deeming animals as *contaminated*; whereas we will usually refer to humans as *infected, ill,* or *sick.*) To reduce the risk of zoonotic infections, the World Health Organization also provides general guidelines. This becomes complex, as concerns about risks to groundwater and soil have to be considered.

In contrast, oceanic beings can usually be left where they die, becoming part of the ocean's banquet of death. Most spectacular are "whale falls," which sink to the seafloor to be consumed by other aquatic life. It's estimated over 70,000 of these large mammals die each year (usually from starvation, injury, or disease).[110] In their death, each supports an ecosystem that marine biologists suggest can last for decades. After a whale is stripped of edible goodies, she becomes a reef habitat.

What about a whale that washes up on a beach? (Perhaps the coast equivalent of that park-based dead moose "near a campsite.") Weighing tons, literally, he may be buried whole, or if that's not possible due to beach size or ocean currents, his immense body may be towed out to sea to become a whale fall. Or he might be carved up into pieces and hauled off to a landfill. The decision will usually be made by the fisheries division of the National Oceanic and Atmospheric Administration (NOAA) due to the Marine Mammal Protection Act.[111]

After one such beaching in Southern California, the Associated Press reported that an onlooker had driven 75 miles to the site to lay an orchid by the whale's body. She also rubbed the whale with homeopathic balms.[112] (Likely well out of sight of folks from the NOAA.)

Usually, though, wildlife deaths rarely receive this care, and certainly not funerary rites. And yet, there are some exceptions to this generalization, where sympathetic humans do have a longstanding tradition of burying wild beings.

For example, in Thailand the Karen people hold funerals for elephants who die nearby their villages. Believing elephants to have spiritual capacities, the Karen seek to assist the animal's *kla* (a word that denotes spiritual life-force) to journey into the next world. Ethnobotanist Alexander M. Greene explains, "The only part of the body which should not be touched after death is the single 'finger' at the end of the trunk, which is believed to have particularly strong *kla* residing in it which could drive away the *kla* of any human who touches it."[113] During the service, the Karen offer prayers for a smooth journey of the elephant's spirit, light candles, and make offerings. Finally, they dig a large grave and reverently bury the massive body.

Wildlife Memorials

The Kootenay National Park (KNP) in southeastern British Columbia is serious about decreasing wildlife mortality in the park as well as memorializing lost lives. On the first count, they've developed ingenious ways to draw drivers' attention to frequent animal routes, such as cutout wood road signs shaped like elk with reflective eyes. The Park also uses fences to guide animals to specially created wildlife overpasses and underpasses in the hope of limiting road crossings.

In 1989, they established a Wildlife Memorial Week, placing notices in local newspapers about the high rate of collisions between vehicles and animals within the park. Then, in 2005, they launched a Highway Wildlife

Mortality Awareness campaign, placing hundreds of flags representing a car-killed animal along the roadway. Of note, KNP representatives surveyed drivers who had passed the installation to determine if this increased awareness would lead to support for decreasing the speed limit in the high-mortality zone. Only 18.8 percent of drivers said they would support reducing the speed limit.[114]

Off highway N2, just north of the Cape Town International Airport, South Africa, a more permanent memorial was conceived by folks frustrated by rampant rhino poaching. The Green Renaissance collective sought to raise awareness of this problem through art. Armed not with rifles but with wire scrubbing brushes and stencils, they created reverse graffiti on the continuous concrete barriers along the motorway. The center of the installation features two rhinoceroses facing each other with a simple message between them in all caps—312 KILLED—representing the number of lives taken that year to date.[115] To amplify impact, the team placed stencils on the barriers and scratched away the black soot underneath to produce a white memorial cross for each of the 312 rhinos. Six months later, they returned to add another 66 crosses. And soon, 245 more, bringing the total to 633 KILLED that year.

Permanent memorial statues are sometimes erected as well for individual animals or species. In the rolling hills of South Dakota, where plentiful live bison once roamed, fourteen bronze creatures now appear—frozen in time, some poised in midair—fleeing from humans on horseback.[116] Just off a beach in Opononi, New Zealand stands a small memorial to Opo the Dolphin, a sea being who inspired regulations protecting dolphins. Beloved by her community but not always treated well, after her mysterious death a local hockey team wore black armbands during one of its games. And while we might be tempted to think this public outpouring of grief is due to current ideals about animal lives, I'll reveal this event took place... in 1956.[117]

Witnessing Wild Losses

As we become more attuned to the lives of others around us, we may become inclined to mark moments when we happen upon a ladybug, spotted turtle, gray squirrel, or red fox that has died. You may already have a blessing, prayer, or mantra for these times. If not, consider if you might like to create one. These needn't be complicated. For example, every time my husband passes an animal killed on the side of the road, he places his right hand over his heart, engaging in a moment of solemn silence. If you are hiking, you might place a small rock cairn by their body. If you are artistic, make a little sketch that you could put in a sacred space in your home.

Reverently witnessing the losses of wild beings means recognizing each animal on this planet as an individual who was once filled with sacred life and connections to other beings who now may be grieving.

If you feel especially moved by wild losses, consider if you might want to become involved with a state park or wildlife preserve near you. Pay them a visit and ask curiously, "How do you bury your dead?" And "Can I help?"

Reflection

WHICH ANIMALS LIVE around me? Whom do I want to know more about? How much do I know about the challenges facing wildlife around my environment? Did I observe any of their deaths in the last week? What was my reaction or action? Were there any deaths for which I was not present but I can infer are still happening around me?

Chapter 9

NOT QUITE WILDLIFE

*I*T WAS PRECISELY 3:47 a.m. South African Standard Time, and I was wide awake. Nervous and excited, I threw on long underwear, cargo pants, winter coat, and fuzzy hat, then opened the door of my rondavel. The sky was remarkably bright with stars. The creatures in the bush were just starting to awake and rustle. Soon, with some luck, I'd be meditating with lions.

Indeed, my husband and I had flown over 8,000 miles due to my lifelong obsession with big cats—ignited by C. S. Lewis's *Chronicles of Narnia*, fanned by *The Lion King*, and stoked by previous trips to Kenya's national parks. Auspiciously, we landed coveted spots to visit a group of white lions who live *not quite wild*, yet *not quite free* in South Africa. Freely roaming on massive plots of land, they reside under human protection and care. On the trip we would learn about lion behavior and conservation, and study cultural connections between local tribal communities and these sacred animals.

That first morning, we headed out in an open-air truck under the tutelage of Jason Turner, a lion ecologist, and Linda Tucker, founder of the Global White Lion Protection Trust. Soon, we stopped a safe distance from a few stunning felines. Our group sat in silence, unmoving. No photos were allowed. No speaking either. No looking the lions in the eye (it can be seen as a challenge). And certainly, no Aslan-style hugging or baby Simba-style *holding over a nearby cliff* action. Instead, we were to observe respectfully, from a distance, attempting to blend into the landscape.

I must admit, there's nothing like connecting with a lion's energy in a mindfulness state. Closing my eyes, I let images interplay, tuning in to my senses: I could smell the grass of the veld and became increasingly aware of the warm thermos of tea at my side. The wind gusted across my face and the heat of the rising sun warmed my back. Then, one lion roared. Suddenly, all the lions I had ever envisioned were present—seemingly (and amusingly) accompanied by the one from the MGM movie-opening credits—all of them belonging to a single omnipresent, eternal Lion.

The encounter was remarkable and a little scary too. Visions flashed before my eyes: the biblical Daniel asleep in the lion's den, the snow lions of Tibetan Buddhist art, and the tragic life of Cecil, a reminder of those killed by trophy hunting.

After a bit, our truck slowly headed out, leaving the big cats to their daily activities. And that's when reality smacked me in the face, disconnecting me from the bliss-filled furry lovefest. Indeed, I was woefully unprepared for the ethical dilemma that appeared through a giant severed giraffe leg abandoned on the dusty ground. I gasped, and my heart sank.

Ensuring managed lions get enough nourishment is complicated since they live within fences. These barriers interfere with normal migration patterns of prey, and thus, humans have to intervene—moving animals from other locales into the lion's environment to become food. And this is the dilemma that knocked me off my feet. Just as I have to make food decisions about the cats in my home, those responsible for captive wild beings have to make daily decisions about who gets eaten. Because these lions, currently, cannot make it on their own in the wild.

Since their "discovery" by humans in 1938, these rare big cats have been hunted, driven from their natural endemic habitat, and denied legal protection. The Global White Lion Protection Trust is working diligently to promote awareness of their plight and raise support for their safety and reintroduction into natural habitats. Following the World Conservation Union's soft-release approach, the Trust introduces lions to progressively larger areas.

Before the lions' release, Linda, Jason, and their staff monitor, study, and care for them. And they answer seemingly endless questions about why humans need to be involved—instead of just letting nature take its course. To these queries, Jason responds, "In reality, there are very few ecosystems today that are not, in some way, 'managed.' Their gene pool in the Kruger National Park was depleted by the lion-culling program in the 1970s. Strictly speaking, then, white lions should rightfully be restored within their natural distribution range. White lions are a unique contribution to the biodiversity of the Greater Timbavati region, and they are culturally significant to indigenous communities in the area. The balance was once disturbed through human intervention, and we need to restore it."[118]

Astute readers may wonder about the implications of humans visiting these lions. While the Global White Lion Protection Trust and other conservation organizations with similar models are careful to limit interactions, I still ponder this myself.

What is the right level of intervention in these animal lives? How do we ensure that intervention does not unfairly affect other species and the welfare of humans at the same time? Of course, these questions aren't limited to lions, elephants, or the countries within Africa.

Animal Ethics in the Wild-*ish*

FOR EXAMPLE, A 2019 study in the journal *Biological Invasions* stated that more than half of the over 400 US National Parks had reported animal species they consider invasive—331 species in all.[119] Sometimes these situations are left alone, and other times, humans intervene. Much of the time, this task falls to the federal government, which manages just over 27 percent of the land in the US, about 640 million acres.[120] It's not all managed by park rangers like Ted, of course. Multiple other agencies are involved, including the Bureau of Land Management, the Fish and Wildlife Service, the Bureau of Reclamation, the US Forest Service, and the Department of Defense. And so, these departments are responsible for deciding if and when to "cull" animals deemed invasive or overpopulated.

The specifics around these events are varied, including promoting natural predation, trapping and transplanting, allowing public hunting or sending out sharpshooters, rounding up animals with the use of helicopters, paying python hunters to shoot large snakes, or "live composting" aquatic life by filling in bodies of water. One ingenious (and frankly, appalling) management strategy for decreasing the population of an invasive lake trout who were wiping out native Yellowstone cutthroat trout included inserting tracking devices into some fish and then tracking them to their spawning sites to kill off their kin.[121] According to the Code of Federal Regulations, the government may also choose to capture, crate, and transport live elk, buffalos, and bears deemed "surplus" from National Parks to game farms or private preserves.[122]

Are these actions helpful stewardship? Or are they cases of humans acting through the lens of dominion to make the world better fit us? Environmental journalist Fred Pearce journeyed across six continents to find out, reporting his conclusions in *The New Wild: Why Invasive Species Will Be Nature's Salvation*. He suggests that far from being nature's destroyers, many demonized alien species can invigorate their resilient environments, transforming the ecological messes humans have made. When protecting species we care about from invaders or acting to promote convenience for humans, he insists we need to acknowledge these acts are for our needs, not for nature's needs. Pearce asserts, "Nature does not exist to do our bidding."[123] Furthermore, he asks us to drop the romanticized view of a pristine, perfectly ordered natural world. Instead, we need to recognize that nature is random, temporary, and constantly changing. In the new wild, he suggests, we often just need to stand back and applaud the invaders, who may just be what the real nature needs.

How Do You Zoo?

SOMETIMES WILD BEINGS are removed from their habitats for humans to use as entertainment. If I were writing this book 30 years ago, I might have launched into a passionate plea now for you to stop taking your kids to the circus by citing abusive trainers, filthy living accommodations, and the hazards of travel. Luckily, in the past few decades, advocate exposés have increased public awareness of the predicaments three-ring staged animals face, leading to increasing local, state, and countrywide bans on their use in entertainment. Circus companies are adapting to new regulations and offering animal-free circuses such as the Bindlestiff Family Cirkus and Cirque du Soleil.

What of zoos and aquariums? While we all might eschew the pitiful concrete roadside attractions that proliferated tourist routes in our youth, modern zoological parks claim not only entertainment but also education and conservation as their mission. How do we assess these claims? And what about "wild" animals who live in sanctuaries?

I admit bewilderment about the ethics regarding animals who live under the care of humans, having observed both seemingly helpful and appallingly horrific conditions. Although the USDA licenses more than 2,800 wildlife exhibitors in the United States, only 223 of them actually meet the requirements for animal welfare, safety, education, and other benchmarks required by the Association of Zoos and Aquariums (A.Z.A).[124] And even those that do seem riddled with problematic reports from animal welfare organizations. A surprising number of captive animals are given Prozac, Celexa, or Haloperidol to deal with the mental stress of their environments.[125] Many develop ingenious methods for escaping their enclosures, a clear case they don't love their digs. Case in point: Emma Marris, in her book *Wild Souls: Freedom and Flourishing in the Non-Human World,* shares the story of a mastermind orangutan housed in the Omaha Zoo who kept a wire for lock-picking hidden within his mouth.[126]

Although many zoos have rebranded themselves as conservational and educational organizations, few actually engage in these activities, and those that do usually prioritize entertainment and profit-making over conservation. The argument that zoos are necessary for animal protection just doesn't add up. If we were to visit a zoo, the challenges for the elephants, primates, and big cats would be readily apparent to us—endlessly pacing, pulling their hair out, self-biting, and so on. And then there's the dreadful detail hidden from most zoo-goers, the common practice of culling (killing) the animals deemed "surplus" at a zoo. Thousands of healthy animals are "euthanized" each year because the zoo doesn't "need" any more of that kind.[127]

And yet, considering there are over 800,000 animals held in A.Z.A. zoos alone, what do we do to improve their lives?

Admittedly, I hold a vision in which all beings are released from captivity to live wild and free in their native habitats. I dream of howler monkeys swinging from rainforest trees, African bush elephants barreling through grassy savannas, and tuxedoed penguins swimming in pristine waters. And yet, this is naïve. Because animals bred in captivity sometimes lack the skills to live wild, world crossing travel is expensive and dangerous, and, perhaps most importantly, if we could get past those challenges, would there actually be any habitat available?

Because, as humans claim more and more of the Earth as ours, we displace animals, which often leads to a choice between their captivity or their death. Tripp York, an American religious studies scholar and Mennonite writer, volunteered at the Virginia Zoo for three years to explore this issue. In his book *The End of Animal Captivity: A Primate's Reflections on Zoos, Conservation, and Christian Ethics*, Tripp concedes,

> Nonintervention is impossible. We intervene constantly—even when we are unaware of it. Whether it is the farmlands that feed us while disrupting the homes of groundhogs; the clear-cutting of forests that spells disaster and extinction of countless animals; the building of roads, tunnels, and bridges that displace innumerable animals; the inadvertent burying of gopher tortoises under construction lots in Florida; or the poaching of rhinos and elephants throughout Africa, human beings are constantly intervening in the lives of animals. There is no hands-off approach. The question is not whether we are going to

intervene; the question is how we are going to intervene.[128]

There is a distressing truthfulness to York's confession. It can be entirely too easy to proclaim that humans should not use or exploit animals. Yet they have been—and continue to be—exploited. What do we do about them? How do we dismantle a socially-normalized system when improving life for one being means greater risk for another? Or when we lack the resources to affect the wide-spread changes that compassionate ethics call for?

Furthermore, how do we engage in interspecies relationships that are fair for all beings involved? Prior to photography, film, and the Internet, zoos were how we learned about animals and how we fed our desire to be amongst other beings. (And for some folks, they stood as a testament of humanity's all-powerfulness as we tamed powerful "beasts.")

Some suggest transforming zoos from the inside out. Others who are aware of the mental and physical health problems of captive animals, suggest a shift to visiting animals in their own location—or at least something approximating it. Does that help?

Interspecies Vacations

VISITING THE LIONS managed by the Global White Lion Protection Trust was not Sean's or my first interspecies vacation. Admittedly, I've trekked the globe searching for experiences with the more-than-human world, from bathing rescued polo elephants in Chitwan, Nepal, to paragliding with vultures in Pokhara, Nepal. Donning scuba gear, I've swum with the angelfish and wrasse along Australia's Great Barrier Reef. I've even hung out with Nemo—or at least one of his distant relatives. Awakening to the sound of howling wolves in New Mexico, Sean zoomed in on our possible retirement location. The thing about animal lovers is that we feel good during these interspecies moments, more alive, more connected.

And yet, there are problematic dimensions when we head out with our cameras in tow, trampling through the brush, stalking "wild" animals to get a glimpse of their majesty and a prized photo to remember them by. Beginning in the early 1900s, animal protection groups urged people to trade their safari guns for new photography technology, and a robust travel infrastructure grew as humans sought the excitement of going hunting not with a gun but with a camera.[129]

Admittedly, this type of travel brings much-needed funding to save endangered and at-risk species as well as fight poaching. At the same time, it also has troublesome aspects as non-African-based interests often appear in tension with the needs of local humans. Caitrin Keiper, former editor of *Philanthropy* magazine, explains,

> To many Westerners, Africa is Eden or the Heart of Darkness, maybe both. To Africans, Africa is where they live. Many see the tremendous foreign interest in, and power brought to bear on protecting their wildlife as just the latest version of imperialism. . . .

It is all very well, it seems, for people whose countries have never dealt with native ele-phants to have the luxury of tooling around in the barren strip malls that support a comfort-able lifestyle and counting on far-off places to hold the soul of the natural world in trust, occasionally piped into our living rooms via nature documentaries—but there are people living there as well, with their own needs and aims and points of view. . . . When sources of income are nearly nonexistent, and there is a voracious if illegal market for elephant prod-ucts, the incentives to ignore the law are far stronger than most local governments' power or resolve to enforce it. [130]

Some animal advocates suggest wildlife photography is tantamount to stalking. Others point to the problems of habitat destruction by tourists. Indeed, we humans often take whatever photos we want to without regard for the rights of the being in the image in an act I suggest could be called *photographic dominion*. On the flip side, wild-life photographers have been critical to raising the public awareness that helped pass the Endangered Species Act.[131]

Photo ethics around image manipulation are partic-ularly heated. Some photographers suggest that photo manipulation can help take pressure off animals and environments by removing the need to interact with them. But, of course, purists grumble. In 1997, the North American Nature Photography Association (ANPA) even issued a "Truth in Captioning" statement suggest-ing that any manipulated photo should be captioned as *Photo Illustration.*[132] Since then, as image editing has become common place, ANPA continues to update their guidelines "to help nature photographers better understand some of the implications of what they're doing."[133]

But some suggest they don't go far enough. Perhaps unrealistically, but honorably, photographer Bill McKibben suggests a moratorium on photographing wildlife due to its potential for harming wildlife habitats. Instead, he asserts there are already plenty of photos in existence, and "wildlife images be pooled and distributed through a central clearinghouse, with strict rules about how new imagery should be created in the future."[134] Amusingly, we now find ourselves in a time where we need to advocate for saving animals from the very process of photography.

Sending Off *Not Quite* Wildlife

ANIMALS IN ZOOS are often given more consideration at death than those who actually live in the wild. I suppose this is because they are known as individuals with names. After the death of the last passenger pigeon, Martha, in 1914, the Cincinnati Zoo renamed one of its aviaries after her kind. The Passenger Pigeon Memorial raises awareness of the once-abundant bird that was hunted into extinction. Martha doesn't reside there, though. Found dead in her cage, she was frozen into a 300-pound block of ice and sent to the Smithsonian, destined for taxidermy and display.[135]

These days, most zoo animals will undergo a necropsy upon death, and pieces of their bodies will be removed for samples to be used in research or education as bio-facts. While a few may end up on display like Martha, the vast majority are incinerated or buried without much fanfare. A high-profile exception was Knut, a polar bear born in captivity at the Berlin Zoological Garden. After being rejected by his mother, Knut captured a worldwide audience as zoo staff pondered what should be done. One die-hard activist suggested the cub should be killed. In response, school children descended upon the zoo with signs declaring "Knut Must Live."[136] Ultimately, zoo humans decided to raise the cub and did so for four years until one day, Knut convulsed in his enclosure and died in front of hundreds of visitors. The public response was profound.

Upon Knut's death, fans showered the zoo's entrance with candles, flowers, photos, notes, and drawings. Their generous donations funded a permanent bronze memorial statue. Knut's body met a controversial fate, though, when his pelt was used to create a full-sized model for Berlin's *Museum für Naturkunde*. A spokesperson for the museum offered, "It's important to make clear we haven't had Knut stuffed. It's an artistically valuable sculpture with the original fur."[137] With respect to the museum, I'm not sure I understand this distinction.

Over at the Seoul Grand Park in Korea, zoo staff performs an annual memorial ceremony to honor the animals that passed within that year. Letters of remembrance are read, and offerings of fruit and flowers are displayed by a massive stone sculpture.[138] Likewise, the Kiryugaoka Zoo in Japan performs memorial services, inviting children from local schools to pay their respects by placing their hands together in a prayer position and offering,

"To them who lived together in the zoo, we pray souls may rest in peace with our deep thanks and respect."[139]

Acknowledging Animal Grief

SOMETIMES, ANIMALS MEMORIALIZE their own losses. Observers have documented complex social behavior concerning death in elephants, dolphins, whales, and chimpanzees.[140] Death practices have also been observed among gorillas, baboons, macaques, lemurs, geladas, giraffes, western scrub jays, buffalo, bears, horses, chickens, and turtles. Notably, chimps, elephants, and magpies engage in behavior that suggests memorialization.[141] Elephants visit the bones of their family members as well as others without a genetic connection.[142] Elephants also seem concerned about deaths beyond their species. They have been observed covering dead rhinos and lions under foliage—as well as a few sleeping humans.[143]

Understanding that animals grieve has profound implications. It suggests that their relationships with each other are incredibly meaningful. Following this thought, we should reflect on the human tendency to separate animal parents from their children or family groups from each other in general. Can we seriously relegate "mating" to something merely biological for them, denying that animal families experience emotions around loss?

Reflection

WHILE SOME OF the stories in this chapter may warm our hearts and others may cause concern, they raise questions worth our contemplation: How many extinct, endangered, vulnerable, or threatened animals can I name? What is my response to the instances of wildlife management and culling described in this chapter? What is our obligation to care for animals who die but aren't under our care? How do I feel about circuses, zoos, animal entertainment, and conservation tourism? What about animals used in movies or social media videos? Can seeking more knowledge about other-than-human grief affect how I feel about animal lives and relationships?

Chapter 10

FARMED AND CORPORATE ANIMALS

"CAN WE GO feed the cows now, Pop-Pop?" my sister Amy and I begged. She was six, and I was eight. We had just tumbled out of the family car after a 1,200-mile ride for our annual visit, bypassing any hello for him or for my grandmother, instead pleading in unison to go see the farm's animals.

My father had long since fled the family farm for a divinity school "up North," yet farm life always remained part of his DNA. So, Amy and I grew up hearing stories about early-morning fieldwork and painful calluses from picking cotton. Driving us to piano lessons, he would reminisce about his disappointment after riding his bike miles along a country trail for a music lesson—only to find that the eggs he had brought for payment had cracked, and thus, there would be no music lesson.

These stories created a thrilling, if not slightly old-fashioned, mythos around the farm. Upon arrival, half a dozen cousins would join us to fight over the crudely constructed treehouse, feed the barn cats, dodge mud daubers in my grandmother's greenhouse, and avoid the underfoot birds who chased us endlessly.

But the highlight of any day was jumping in the cargo bed of my grandpa's baby-blue, step-side, pickup truck to toss out hay bales. As we barreled along, honking loudly across the pasture, the cattle mooed. At each stop, they nuzzled our tiny, outstretched hands. After that, we'd replace salt licks and head to the barn to slop pigs. We were then freed to play until a clang on the porch bell summoned us all for dinner.

Paradoxically, I never recall connecting anything we did during the day with what appeared on our dinner plates. I suspect this was partly because my grandmother usually fed us canned SPAM or fried chicken, not beef. And as I recall, our plates were mostly filled with the okra, corn, green beans, and cantaloupe they grew—whatever happened to be "in season"—followed by a lot of sweets. Grandma was famous for her spongy jelly rolls and delicious layered cakes. On rainy days, we'd spend hours learning the finer points of baking until she tired of our presence and called Pop-Pop over to chase us through the farmhouse's swinging doors with a fly swatter.

Embarrassingly, I was 19 before realizing the farm's animals were not the same ones continuously throughout my youth. I simply had never thought about it. To me, farms had cows and pigs like our house had cats. My grandfather's animals always seemed healthy and happy, not in distress. Plus, I had never witnessed one being killed. In hindsight, if one did end up as dinner, the linkage was never discussed.

My *aha!* moment came one Thanksgiving during

college when I visited my boyfriend's family home. It was a farm-ish place, sporting a large vegetable garden, a single cow named Bessie, a beagle dog whose name I can't recall, and tons of squirrels. The meal was off to a rough start for me. Nervous about meeting his family members for the first time, I listened—frozen—as they laughed about popping squirrels with a BB gun out the kitchen window. Soon, the topic moved on to deer hunting. I poured another glass of wine to steady my discomfort. Finally, an uncle asked my boyfriend's father, "So, when you gonna slaughter Bessie?" I fled the table.

My boyfriend found me in the kitchen, and as I recall, asked incredulously, "What's the problem? Where do you think yesterday's hamburgers came from?" He then explained that his family raised an ongoing string of solitary cows who ended up in their garage's big, white freezer, packaged and labeled by a local butcher. To my protests about slaughtering the family pet, he explained, "It's not a pet. And it's much tastier and healthier than what you are buying in the grocery store. At least I know where my food comes from!" I asserted my concern for Bessie, "How cruel to make an animal trust you and then kill it!" And, to this, he dropped the bomb, "Well, your grandfather does it too."

My journey since then—to reconcile my compassion and love for animals with my diet and lifestyle choices— has been, and remains, a messy one. Growing up with positive memories of a family farm led me to believe naïvely that all farms were like that—caring people who loved animals they knew personally. I was woefully undereducated about the growing problems in animal agriculture. But I was willing to learn.

What's the Problem with Farming Animals?

SHOCKINGLY, MOST FARMS like my grandfather's are gone. Instead, here is what farming now looks like: "First, there are over 100 billion farmed animals alive at this moment—more than 10 times the number of humans. Second, over 90 percent (over 99 percent in the US) of these animals live on industrial, large-scale 'factory farms' enduring atrocious cruelty, such as intense confinement in tiny cages, brutal mutilation and slaughter methods, and rampant disease and suffering from artificial breeding for excessive production of meat, dairy, and eggs."[144]

Upon reading this description, most carnivores, omnivores, flexitarians, vegetarians, and vegans alike must acknowledge that there is something amiss. How did this happen?

Indeed, farmers like my grandfather rarely exist anymore either. Corporate agribusiness has devastated farming families, rural communities, and the environment. Pesticides and fertilizers pollute waterways and damage soil. Foul-smelling excrement wafts through the air in many rural communities. Increased use of hormones and antibiotics leads to health problems for animals and humans alike. Pandemics and epidemics lead to the tragic destruction of millions of animal lives. Furthermore, all these symptoms of a system way out of balance place unimaginable stress on farmworkers who experience trauma from and grief over the treatment of beings in their care and the losses they witness. This grief is usually deemed "unacceptable" within their community and, thus, remains unaddressed.

Psychiatrist and grief researcher Anna Chur-Hansen

reveals that farming practices such as killing and culling can result in PTSD, suicidal thoughts, and "feelings of guilt, regret, shame, helplessness, anger, grief, anguish, and a sense of failure." What's more, it can affect their families. Chur-Hansen reflects, "It may be particularly devastating when the animals are healthy and must be destroyed due to drought or lack of feed. Animals that the children in the family viewed as pets may have to be destroyed during epidemics, again a most distressing experience."[145] Another concern Chur-Hansen raises is cultural. "Families may have bred the animals over many generations, thus, having to destroy them may be symbolic of an end to a proud heritage and tradition of bloodlines. The loss of the animals may mean economic failure and the consequent loss of the farm or property, which again may have been handed down through a number of generations. Culling livestock usually affects the individual, their families, and their wider community, as well as society as a whole."[146]

I wish my grandfather were still alive. How I long to ask him so many questions. What challenges did he face? Did he ever have questions about what was on his dinner plate? Would he have been interested in transitioning his farm to a plant-based one that was devoid of killing? What would he think about new options for lab-grown meat from animal cells that avoid hormones, antibiotics, bacterial contamination, and slaughter? And deep down, I ache to find out where the cows went when they left his farm—to ask if he ever had to "destroy" cows himself due to economic challenges or disease? And if so, how did that impact his life?

Consumers who eat farmed animals are rarely aware that their decision affects not only the animal who will be used for food, but also the people who raised the animal. These consequences aren't ones most people would think about when ordering a hamburger or picking up a steak at a grocery store. We don't want to think about the suffering in agriculture, do we?

The costs animals and humans pay in the name of our current "food system" are likely to become even more pressing. The COVID-19 pandemic increased worldwide awareness of the link between animal farming and disease. Yet, many people may be surprised to hear that outbreaks happen all the time. One research report reveals, "nearly 55,000 outbreaks of animal disease were reported to the World Animal Health Information Database between 2005 and 2016."[147] These outbreaks aren't random, either. They are the result of modern animal agriculture practices and the consumer preferences that drive them.

Yet, merely switching to plant-based agriculture won't solve all the problems.

I recently spent some time noodling the topic with Aline Silva, a local parish pastor who has served rural and farming populations for over a decade. She pointed out another layer of complexity. Silva explained, "The issue stretches beyond a single country's borders. While many of us may endeavor to shop local, the vast majority of our food is shipped to our local stores, often traveling surprisingly long distances." Silva continued, "As a first-generation immigrant of Brazil to the United States, being in the work of advocacy for the welfare of animals also means caring for my community. Brazil is one of the largest producers of cattle for beef in the world (second only to China). Our relationship with raising animals for food has a long history. It affects not only our daily diet but also the deforestation of the Amazon, the displacement of millions of indigenous people, and endangers a lot of protected species as well. When my people become displaced, it's an issue of concern for me."[148]

In response to these entangled issues, Silva became the codirector of CreatureKind, a nonprofit that helps farming communities explore animal welfare issues through faith-based theo-ethics. One core goal is helping communities reduce the use of animal products in favor of consuming more plant-based foods that are less resource-intensive. (For example, water is a big deal. It takes a lot more to create a pound of animal-based meat than it takes to grow vegetables, grains, and beans. On average, it takes 1,800 gallons of water to produce a single pound of meat!)[149]

An increasing number of both religious and secular people who are passionate about food justice, point to these entangled food problems that extend beyond animal welfare, such as *food justice* (the right for all people to have food), *food sovereignty* (including the right for local growers not to be overshadowed by multinationals), and combating *food insecurity* (by determining more equitable distribution of food).

One way to mitigate some of these challenges is to change default choices for food in cafeterias, spiritual communities, and other group settings to plant-based ones—referred to as DefaultVeg. If this idea has you feeling uncomfortable, ask yourself this, "Why is the default main course often animal meat?" Some people tell me that we should default to what "the majority" eat. But we've seen in other areas of our lives how privileging dominant culture is a problem, so that can't really stand as a good rationale! Plus, there are some compelling data to consider. One poll suggested that 46 percent of US adults always or sometimes eat plant-based meals when eating out.[150] So eating meat at every meal is hardly the norm.

Yet, becoming plant-forward or plant-based won't solve all of the issues in our agriculture system. We have to look at what we eat from the widest possible perspective. For example, Silva points to this paradox: the places that grow our food regularly experience food insecurity. "Approximately 75 percent of field workers were born south of the US border, and they are responsible for feeding most of the people in North America. The vast majority of field workers are people of color living in rural, low-income communities. The places working so hard to grow our food to feed America are having a hard time feeding themselves and being economically supported."[151] Creating equitable food systems means considering all the beings involved—not merely deciding to eat vegetarian or vegan. While that can be a good start to reducing the suffering of farmed animals, we must also work diligently to reduce the suffering for human animals as well.

Is it Time to Rethink Eating Meat?

ADMITTEDLY, THERE IS a tension between welfarist and abolitionist approaches to solving the problems in our food system. Welfarists want to improve conditions for the animals stuck in the farm system, sometimes seeing this as a first step towards animal-free farming. Abolitionists want to completely remove animals from the system.

For example, in the United Kingdom, the University of Chester has published a robust resource, *The Christian Ethics of Farmed Animal Welfare: A Policy Framework for Churches and Christian Organizations,* offering faith-based reasons for why farmed animal welfare should be considered as part of Christian living.[152] Notably, their document steers clear of moral considerations, instead taking what is often referred to as a *welfarist approach.* The authors state, "This framework does not address the question of whether animals should be farmed. It does not engage with Christian arguments for vegetarianism or veganism, positively or negatively. Instead, it recognizes that animals are being farmed, that they are likely to be for the foreseeable future, and that different ways of farming animals have very different impacts on their flourishing and the flourishing of farmers, farmworkers, rural communities, and wider human communities."[153]

In contrast, the Interfaith Vegan Coalition (IVC)—while also concerned about animals flourishing—has a definitive position on whether animals should be farmed: *No.* Combining the forces of independent individuals and two-dozen organizations that represent diverse religions and wisdom traditions, the IVC envisions a world where animals are neither farmed nor exploited but rather treated with compassion and respect, including liberation from captivity and exploitation.[154]

Member groups include the American Vegan Society, Catholic Action for Animals, Jewish Veg, Catholic Concern for Animals, Christian Vegetarian Association, Climate Healers, Quaker Animal Kinship, Dharma Voices for Animals, St. Francis Alliance, Vegan Spirituality, and many more. The IVC's "religion-specific advocacy kits" provide downloadable resources to help religious and spiritual communities align scriptural and heart-centered values—such as love and compassion—with worship practices, holiday rituals, prayers, and community activities.[155]

And there's also the Animal Interfaith Alliance, another umbrella organization of faith-based animal advocacy groups centered in the UK that includes various Anglican, Buddhist, Catholic, Hindu, Jain, Jewish, Quaker, and Unitarian groups, including Animals in Islam and the International Ahimsa Organisation. If you are interested in learning more about how animal-loving people are raising concerns about the exploitation of animals in their religious communities, these organizations are a great way to get actionable ideas.

Another innovative program seeking to tackle the problems of animal agriculture is the Rancher Advocacy Program (RAP), which offers support, encouragement, and resources for ranchers to turn their land into environmental and animal friendly farms. RAP helps cattle ranchers or animal farming families who want to transition from animal agriculture to a "financially stable, environmentally-friendly way of life while preserving their culture and history."[156] Acknowledging the emotional conflict these families face, RAP helps animal farmers stop farming animals and transition to farming solar or wind energy, plant-based vegan agriculture, and other creative ideas. Likewise, a few animal-friendly organizations help dairy farmers convert from cow-milk to plant-milk operations, removing the problematic actions of artificially inseminating cows or separating moms and babies.

Becoming Willing to See

WHILE THE ANIMAL farming industry was transforming from private to corporate, and from seen to hidden, I became an adult. I had no idea about the stress that my animal-farming grandparents might be going through. Furthermore, I had no clue about what farmed animals were going through. Or did I?

In hindsight, I made sure to buy "dolphin-safe tuna" (slyly deceived into valuing the lives of one sea-dweller over another). And I recall purposely avoiding the "meat aisle" most of the time. What I bought in stores or ordered at restaurants bore minimal resemblance visually to animals—like beef tacos, sweet-and-sour chicken, and so on. On the dairy side, I was seduced by manipulative packaging design, promising cruelty-free eggs and slick milk ads that bragged about the supposedly happy cows living in California. Interestingly, I freely bought leather motorcycle jackets and down comforters without a second thought about how they were created.

These remembrances tell me I must have sensed dissonance. I was thinking about my purchasing choices—but not consistently. I can see I had more concern for some animal lives over others. Yet, slowly, my awareness increased, one issue at a time.

As a result, I'm quite ticked off at companies that hide the abuses of these animals while wrecking our planet and flooding our stores with deceptive packaging that made me think I was actually making a difference. And I'm even angrier about "Ag-gag" laws which prevent people from investigating these companies. I'm downright enraged that most so-called "animal welfare" laws do not include farmed animals or ocean beings. I think you also might be surprised at what is going on under our noses. Because we're not callous. We're just ignorant on this topic.

For example, a 2014 US study found that 95 percent of respondents were concerned about farmed animal welfare, 93 percent felt it was very important to buy meat from humane sources, and 76 percent were willing to pay more for "humanely-raised" meat.[157] Perhaps even more interestingly, a survey just a few years later revealed that 75 percent of US adults believe they usually eat meat, dairy, and eggs "from animals that are treated humanely."[158]

Yet only a fraction actually do, since over 99 percent of animals that are farmed in the US live on concentrated animal feeding operations (CAFOs) in horrific conditions, with very little concern for their welfare.[159] The numbers just don't add up—humane meat simply does not exist at the quantity we think it does. (And many would argue combining the words "humane and meat" is simply a sleight of hand anyway.) It's just not possible tactically. There is not enough land available on Earth to humanely raise free roaming animals at the quantity people want. And so, if we care about the shape of the planet, about people not going hungry, and about animals not being exploited, we need to look very carefully at what we are consuming and see if we'd be willing to make some changes.

Admittedly, within the scope of this book, I'm not going to elaborate further on how to do that. Nor am I going to proclaim what decisions I think you should make about what you eat, wear, or use. Not because I don't care. I do—*a lot*. But because other authors have already written informative and helpful books to help you figure that out, such as Jonathan Saffran Foer's *Eating Animals*; A. Breeze Harper's *Sistah Vegan: Black Female Vegans Speak on Food, Identity, Health, and Society*; Gene Baur's *Farm Sanctuary: Changing Hearts and Minds About Animals and Food*; and Victoria Moran's *The Good Karma Diet: Eat Gently, Feel Amazing, Age in Slow Motion*. And for those of you who were intrigued by the sentence I slipped in about cell-cultured meat a couple of pages back, I highly recommend Jacy Reese's *The End of Animal Farming: How Scientists, Entrepreneurs, and Activists Are Building an Animal-Free Food System*. Indeed, Jacy insists that the end of animal farming does not need to be the end of meat. So, if you are a meat-loving animal lover, I think you're going to be interested in Jacy's forward-looking perspective.

What I am going to suggest we do in this chapter is acknowledge our interconnection with farmed and other corporate animals. I want us to get really curious about things we do on autopilot and consider any changes we might be willing to make to improve the lives and deaths of these beings. Over 60 percent of the mammals living on Earth are farmed. In fact, there are nine states in the US where cattle outnumber people.[160] In Nebraska, where I lived as a kid, the ratio is 3:1, and in South Dakota, it's even higher. In Iowa and North Carolina there are more pigs than humans, with ratios as high as 29:1 in some counties.[161]

I challenge us to ask, "Why do we self-proclaimed animal lovers find it more difficult to consider these lives than those of the dogs and cats in our homes?"

Reflection

IF YOU HAVE a few minutes, try this exercise. Grab a piece of paper and a pen. Now, make a list of all the beings you encounter as part of your life and ones that might be invisible to you but that we've contemplated in this book. You can use broad categories or, to really explore, use specific species. Some ideas for inclusion: Spouse/partner, wildlife in your yard, family members, people you work with, zoo animals, your inlaws, dogs used in medical research, cows, salmon, people who live in other countries, people in your political party, people in other political parties, deer, people you go to school with, mice, and so on.

Now, draw a large circle. In the center, write "Me." Plot everyone else from your list into the circle based on how much concern you have for their well-being. Those you feel closest to should be plotted near you in the center of the circle. Those you don't care about so much should be plotted further out towards the circle's borderline.

If you meet resistance about judging others, think critically about this. Though we may want to cling to thinking, "I treat all beings with equal compassion!" it's darn near impossible. While that may be our aspiration, it is probably not the truth. While we can have moral regard for all beings, it is likely we have more for some than others, revealed in the ways we act toward them.

Avoid critiquing your process. This reflection is not about judging ourselves as good or bad, but instead about collecting information to become more aware of the biases and socialized ideas that we hold. As a final step, jot down a few words about how it feels to make this inquiry.

Why We Struggle

ADMITTEDLY, THIS EXERCISE can be frustrating. Some of you may just skip it altogether, for fear it might reveal that you are not nearly as compassionate as you may aspire to be. That's okay. That acknowledgement is information in itself. It's important to be gentle with ourselves when we observe and challenge our existing beliefs.

As we explored in Chapter 4, one impediment to treating all species with equal compassion is how we have been socialized about what different animals are *for.* Another factor is our distance from these beings, especially in the case of animals used for food and fashion who are purposely hidden from us in immense windowless buildings that don't even register on our radar.

Another big piece of the puzzle seems to be how we use sentience to rationalize our choices. In general, to be sentient is to have awareness and be capable of feeling; although, admittedly, the term remains slippery and nuanced. *Who* is sentient? How do we prove it? Are there levels of sentience?

While most of us have kicked Descartes' *automata* to the curb, acknowledging that animals are not mechanistic, we are still taught to think of some species with abstraction. This allows us to act as if these beings lack individual personalities of their own. We may view them as a means-to-an-end product. People who work with them may often assign these creatures numbers rather than names. All of these factors distance us from our natural ability to empathize.[162] Viewing animals in a detached way, we deny that they understand what is happening to them and dismiss their capacity to have opinions and feelings about their treatment. In other words, we will grant dogs and cats rich mental lives but not extend this capability to cows, chickens, salmon, and goats. Researchers who study how we value other beings call this attribute *mind perception*, and it has a strong influence on our judgments, such as whether animals are considered food items or treated with moral deservingness.[163]

Think about it for a moment. We do the same thing to people. Judgment underlies sexism, genderism, racism, and perhaps most obviously, ableism. How we evaluate someone's mental abilities—human or other species—has historically been used as a way to deny individuals and groups rights. Furthermore, it decides who we will extend compassion to and whether we will place the needs of others over our own personal interests, including the needs of our planet.

Scholars increasingly point to the intersection of issues that create systemic injustice on an interspecies scale—we cannot completely segregate animal issues from human ones. Problems appear in tandem. So, how do we start untangling them? I believe the first step is to critically dig into our *moral circles* (or *moral expansiveness circle*), the name for the diagram you created in the reflection.

In general, most humans follow a typical pattern, with some variation based on cultural factors. Below is a sample of a moral circle from a research study published in the *Journal of Personality and Social Psychology*. The authors explain, "People have a tendency to put their family and friends at the center of their moral circle, with other human groups afforded lower levels of priority. In-group members are more central than out-group members, followed by highly sentient animals, the environment, animals with low sentience, and plants. (Villains, interestingly, often lie outside people's moral circles altogether.)"[164]

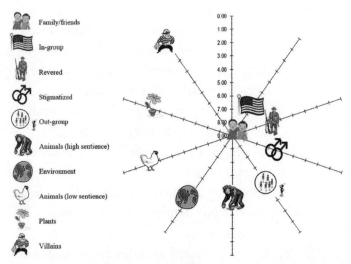

Figure 1. "Normative pattern of entities on the Moral Expansiveness Scale, with more central positions indicating greater moral concern." Charlie R. Crimston, Paul G. Bain, Matthew J. Hornsey, and Brock Bastian. "Moral Expansiveness: Examining Variability in the Extension of the Moral World." *Journal of Personality and Social Psychology* 111, no. 4 (October 2016): 636–53. DOI:10.1037/pspp0000086

The further out someone is on our moral expansiveness circle, the more likely we'll be okay with them being used. Applying this to nonhuman species goes like this: If we consider an animal to have a high level of sentience—like a golden retriever—we will care about them more than a being we judge to have a lower level of sentience—for example, a turkey. The more moral consideration we have for a being, the more likely we will feel obligated to rescue it from suffering. Conversely, lack of moral obligation leads to us being ok with using sentient beings as products, test subjects, or imprisoned workers. We will also be more likely to call a being *it*. Accordingly, lack of moral compassion and obligation is how baby cows become belts or shoes and how more than 65,000 dogs find themselves confined to laboratories to be fed poisonous chemicals or be unnecessarily operated on.[165] Or why 100 million animals—from mice to dogs, cats, monkeys, fish, and birds—will suffer horrific deaths in labs each year in the US alone.[166]

Of course, concern for others varies widely based on the culture and community that one lives in. In some countries, a dog is food; in others, a dog is a companion. One person may resist killing an animal for religious reasons, while another will serve up that animal for dinner without a second thought. A vegan might avoid purchasing a leather sofa, but a hunter might have no compunction about mounting an entire animal in their living room. As I've noted multiple times so far, the beliefs that led to these decisions developed over decades through socialization. Thus, whether someone would consider a nonhuman animal worthy of moral consideration is highly influenced by invisible ideological frameworks. Of course, no one ever gives us a handy moral circle diagram telling us how to make those decisions. Instead, we create one over years and decades.

Digging into our beliefs doesn't mean blaming ourselves for the choices we've made when our compassion starts to expand in new ways toward other beings. Nor does it mean shaming or punishing others when their circles don't match ours.

Yet, if we consider ourselves animal lovers, we must have the courage to analyze why we might act in ways that are absent of love to some animals. Likewise, if we consider ourselves compassionate people, we need to explore the limits of where we place compassion. Let's start from the outside in.

Let's Talk About Villains

DID ANY VILLAINS show up on your circle? The researchers from the study I referenced above suggested that we tend to place villains at the outer edge of our circle because we think they deserve punishment. (Aha! So, that explains why I care about rodents more than Darth Vader. But, alas, the decisions we make about who we prioritize are no laughing matter.)

The sheer existence of villains is also socialized. From Darth Vader to the Joker to the Wicked Witch of the West, and so on, children are raised with stories that suggest what should be done to people who act in mean, power hungry, or violent ways. Of course, the recent proliferation of origin stories for bad guys (and bad gals to a lesser extent) bears witness that we are aware that villains are complex. Peering back through their histories, we learn about the formative experiences that make them who they are. We see through their eyes and learn to empathize, even if we still disagree with their moral choices.

During the 2019 pandemic, I binge-watched *Gotham*, a series based on characters from the Batman franchise.[167] Prequel-ish, the episodes explore the origins of notorious villains such as the Penguin and the Riddler, well before Bruce Wayne became the Dark Knight. Notably, while

I recall rooting against these notorious bad guys as a kid, they have now stolen my heart. Rather than cast as evil—presumably so the hero can become savior—the series reveals these characters' tragic roots, broken dreams, and unrequited loves. So much so that I admit, I want to hug the Penguin. And pay for therapy for the Riddler. So, when looking at my own moral circle, I now ask myself these questions: *What would it take to overcome my biases about people I cast as villains or judge as enemies? What might I learn if I went past calling them out on social media and tried to understand the back story that leads them to do what I find troubling?*

Of course, the more I ponder this, the more the Universe gives me an opportunity to find out. Soon, circumstances found me traveling by the farm my grandfather once owned, which had been out of our family since his death. A sign appeared on the fence announcing the new owners were operating a small cattle company. Thanks to Google, I soon had a phone number and texted the residents to ask whether it might be possible for me to stop by. An answer soon appeared, "Yes. What was your grandfather's name?" After I answered, another text pinged, "We have been told how nice he was."

Through a series of texts, we decided I would stop by the next day. And that's when the pit in my stomach appeared. Plant-based eater and animal lover that I am, what business did I have going to a cattle farm? What was I going to say to them? Would I see the cows and just break down in tears? Would I have the courage to ask them the questions I wanted to ask my grandfather: *Why are you doing this? How can you handle loving these animals and knowing they will be killed? Do you artificially inseminate your cows, and if so, do you really think that's okay? Does it break your heart to separate the babies from their mothers? What about when you have to send them away?* That night I dreamed of infamous animal activist Joaquin Phoenix. I awoke amused at how my mind had perfectly conjured up this *Joker villain meets animal rescuer.*

When I arrived, a woman met me with a big smile. *Whew,* I thought. *She clearly did not Google me.* We had a friendly chat about the barn that was still standing from the days of my grandfather, as I recalled how my parents had spent a whole summer repainting it. Rolling down memory lane, I reflected on how my cousins and I would play for hours on its upper floor, jumping from hay bale to hay bale until someone got stung by a wasp, and we had to rush back to our parents to be triaged. I noted that the original farmhouse was gone, as were all the other makeshift sheds I remembered from my youth and the treehouse that we kids fiercely fought over.

Yet, in the pasture were Black Angus beings like the ones I remembered. Lying in the midst of miles and miles of farm fencing, munching on grass, mooing, and thinking about—well, I don't know, and I really wanted to. Soon, her husband pulled up in his truck, and after some traditional Southern greetings, a two-hour tour of the farm commenced. The couple pointed out the areas they had improved and the places a recent tornado had caused damage on fencing. They introduced me to their cattle and answered my plentiful inquiries and follow-ups, which I tried to ask objectively. I was here to ask questions. I would sort out my emotions later.

Although we didn't speak directly about our positions on animal issues, it was clear that they were different.

At one moment, I couldn't help but confess my love for squirrels. At another, they shared about hunting on the land. I confessed that I had been quite unaware of the goings-on of the farm as a child and felt some confusion about why we didn't talk about the killings and cullings and how I was in my twenties before I realized the cattle were not pets.

I felt like I had enrolled in an experiential course titled Cattle 101. Some of the lessons bothered me, especially those about artificial insemination. As someone who has survived nonconsensual sexual contact, I am not a fan of anyone touching another without consent.

Strikingly, I was impressed by the emotion in their voices as they described how they cared for the cattle. I listened as the wife described how she intuited when a calf was about to be born each time she saw a pregnant cow start to separate herself from the others and seek the shade of a tree during the day.

Although each being had the typical number fastened to their ear, a few also had names. I was struck by how both the husband and wife straddled a line of deeply caring for these animals while also seeing them as products and part of a business. I was perplexed about how they were able to hold both of these views at the same time (a phenomenon that has been labeled as *doubling*).[168]

At the end of the tour, I was shown where they planned to build a new home. My tour guides shared proudly that they were building the business as a legacy for their two young sons. As we took one last look at the beautiful cattle chilling under a shady tree, the husband offered, "They look happy, don't they?" He gave me a final lesson about antibiotics and other hot topics in animal agriculture, and

I could sense as he spoke that he had indeed known my position about animals throughout the afternoon, after all. "They have a great life with us here," he said, "followed by one really bad day."[169] My heart sank.

As we rejoined his wife by the farm's entrance, he shared his frustration with how farmers are treated as villains and people who hurt animals. Instantly, at that moment, I felt pain in my feet. The wife reacted instantly, pulling individual fire ants off my sneakers and pants. For a moment, I thought perhaps the ants were advocating on behalf of the cattle, biting me as penance for not rescuing the cattle all around me. The husband picked up one of the larger winged ants, observing it as it crawled across his index finger. "This one's a queen," he remarked.

After having mothered me, his wife jumped into the conversation, saying that she hoped people wouldn't treat their boys poorly and say bad things about them being farmers, as they really loved the cattle too. He, looking at the ant on his finger, reflected, "One of the boys wants to be a myrmecologist. He loves ants," then placed the queen gently down onto the ground.

Soon after, we parted ways: they headed out back to their chores while I headed out the red dirt road for a long drive, simultaneously feeling the warmth that comes from connecting with strangers and profound sadness over the context of the moment. It is much easier to villainize people who are violently abusing animals in front of you than it is to condemn people acting from what they experience as love.

I worried that some of my friends would see this encounter as being complicit in animal exploitation. Yet, unlike Joaquin Phoenix, I do not have instant access to a cattle truck. So, instead, I signed up for training with the Rancher Advocacy Program's Summit, to learn how I can speak effectively and compassionately to the couple about my concerns. And I made a silent promise to those cattle that I would talk to their people about transitioning to an animal-free farm.

Sending Off Corporate Animals

OUR MORAL CIRCLES affect not only how we treat living beings. They also affect how we treat people and animals when they die. Perhaps unsurprisingly, the further someone is from the center of our moral circle, the less likely we may be to mourn them. While we may memorialize and mourn a friend or family member, and increasingly the dogs, cats, and other species who live in our homes, most of us don't perform these actions for the animals who get eaten or worn. (There are a few exceptions, and we'll look at those in a bit.)

Consumers rarely mourn, grieve, or memorialize what ends up on their dinner plate. Likewise, many animal farmers avoid inquiring into the fate of beings they have raised once the animals leave their farm. The deaths of farmed animals are usually not memorialized. For the most part, instead, we have developed ingenious methods for easing any discomfort about the deaths of beings for whom we have some, but not strong, moral regard.

Saying Grace

This past Thanksgiving, I had my usual anguish over well-meaning people sending me photos of happy turkeys saying, "Gobble! Gobble!" My inner sassy troublemaker wanted to respond, "What part of me being an animal lover do you not understand?!" Yet, I took a deep breath and remembered how deeply entrenched carnism—the invisible ideology that eating animal meat should be the norm, and that those who do not eat animal meat are abnormal—is within our society.

So, I answered their texts as gently as I could, in hopes that next year perhaps they'd send a vegetable-filled cornucopia to me instead—well, most of the messages. One really got me thinking. An animated GIF arrived with an avatar of one of my students, knife in one hand, fork in the other, getting ready to attack a cooked turkey. Across the bottom, it said, "Happy Thanksgiving." What surprised me was that I knew this student had taken Bodhisattva vows in the Tibetan Mahāyāna Buddhist tradition. Although I'm not sure of the exact words he vowed, in general, I knew they would have taken some form of "May I attain Buddhahood for the benefit of all sentient beings." And so, I wondered how a dead turkey reconciled with a vow to benefit all beings. Since he and I have a good rapport, often filled with snark and bad jokes, I responded, "Um, I've got a bit to say about that image. #bodhisattvathanksgiving." He quickly countered, "It was a roadkill. I thanked him for his sacrifice and assured him his death will not go to waste. I also prayed he has a more fortunate rebirth with better vision and quicker moves."

In his tongue-in-cheek statement, I noticed a few things. First, a focus on efficiency. My student was clear to state he had not killed the animal for food but was eating it so that the life would not be wasted. Next, there was gratitude. He had been thankful. Third, he had wished for the animal to have a good life after death. Through each one of these statements, he seemed to be acknowledging moral concern. Granted, he had not intended the GIF to be an ethical discourse for me to analyze, and yet, his text told me a lot about his beliefs. It also exposed my bias toward thinking all Buddhists should be vegetarian, based on my understanding of the first of five precepts that underlie Buddhist ethics: "I observe, refraining from killing any living beings."

Buddhist ethics are complicated. As we keep seeing over and over how ethics become actions, even within spiritual traditions, humans are not consistent. Dharma Voices for Animals (DVA) suggests that the inconsistency about eating animals within different lineages of Buddhism exists because of variations in the texts used for guidance, explaining, "The question of eating animals is addressed at length in several Mahāyāna sutras, and the prohibition is clear and unequivocal. In the *Laṅkāvatāra Sūtra*, the Buddha offers numerous reasons to abstain from eating animals and continually reaches the same conclusion: the Bodhisattva, whose nature is compassion, is not to eat any animal flesh."[170] At the same time, DVA suggests that the Pali canon used in Theravadan Buddhism provides less direct guidance in this area and leaves a lot of room for exceptions.[171]

Shortly after the turkey text from my student, I received a text from a Christian family member proclaiming,

"Thanking God today for all that I am able to receive and the ability I have to give. And for the turkey who gave its life for my lunch today!" This sentiment of an animal "giving its life" seems particularly prevalent in before-meal graces I hear from my Christian friends—that somehow the animal had given itself for food. I presume this is a halo effect off of Jesus, who, according to their soteriological viewpoint, "gave up" his life. I usually point out that the turkey did no such thing. He had no agency in the decision. In moments like these, I can't help myself. I ask, "Just how, exactly, did the turkey give his life?" Seriously, I am not the person you want to invite to Thanksgiving dinner.

When questioned about the issue of eating animals within Christianity, I'm likely to launch into a passionate speech noting Chapter 36 of the Rule of St. Benedict required monks (except for the sick) to abstain from meat. Many influential theologians were plant-forward, including Clement of Alexandria, Origen, and Tertullian, who wrote that the eating of flesh blocked spiritual awareness.[172] Really on a roll, I'll reveal the Essenes, Desert Fathers, Cistercians, Carthusians, Trappists, and Orthodox monks have all encouraged what we now call vegetarianism either to become closer to God or for ethical reasons. I may even tell you the Pythagorean Greeks and Egypt's priestly class did too.[173] You'd be right to presume that I don't get many Easter dinner invitations either.

Questioning the Gratitude Bypass

It's not that I mean to be trouble or a bad house guest, but I am seriously perplexed at how saying we are *grateful* somehow helps the animals. My willing-to-tussle friends will advise me that the words of their meal grace are intended not toward the animals but to show their gratitude for the food. Which I understand on an intellectual level. Around the world, over 690 million people do not have enough to eat.[174] Hunger, food insecurity, and food injustice are real issues and deserve much more attention than they receive.

At the same time, I can't help but think that terminology of gratitude and sacrifice can be used as a convenient excuse to view carnism from a one-sided perspective—that of humans. Prayer over food is common to many religions, of course. A recent study suggested over 50 percent of American households "say grace."[175] Yet, from an interspecies perspective, these words do little to lessen the pain animals incur in our food system. Furthermore, kosher and halal principles are still about slaughtering and do not remove the fear and anguish those beings experience. And so, I think, those who choose to eat animal meat need to be careful with words, avoiding implying that the animal gave itself or sacrificed itself to be food.

Now, some may argue with me here, citing age-old stories such as Tale 316 of the Buddhist *Jataka Tales,* in which a rabbit flings itself into the fire of an old man begging for food. Or that other rabbit who offers itself to the god Quetzalcoatl. My science-loving friends may cite beings that allow their offspring to feed on them if they cannot find food, such as Caecilians or pseudoscorpions. My Buddhist student might agree with me on eschewing narratives of sacrificial offerings, suggesting that his blessings and meal rituals indeed benefit animals by helping them reincarnate as higher beings with increased merit.

And so, it's simply impossible to separate eating from our spiritual beliefs—they are entangled.

Dr. Emily Bailey studies the long-standing linkage of religion with food and suggests why narratives about eating remain influential. "Shared food identity largely stems from individual and collective food memories, and is reinforced by commensality, or the practice of eating together," she observes. "Food memories are therefore largely responsible for shaping cuisine, informing eating behaviors and dining etiquette, dictating taste, and creating systems of power. This is especially pronounced in religious food practices, which intentionally invoke nostalgia in the process of creating spiritual meals."[176] Bailey also notes that systematic approaches to food within religions also guide exceptions. Ritual is used to make forbidden things permissible or to provide acceptable context for eating actions. I suspect this may be why many place so much power in the idea of saying grace.

It's striking that we don't extend these rituals beyond dinner plates. For example, I don't hear people give thanks for the cow parts in their collagen face cream, the pig parts in their floor wax or shaving cream, the rendered horse fat in their Downy detergent, or the herring scales in their nail polish. Of course, to be fair, they probably didn't realize these products were made from animals. But it's unbelievable how many "rendered" dead animal bodies go into beauty and home products. Indeed, many of us have really only been conditioned to say grace *when we are eating*. Notably, some of my Jewish friends say over 100 blessings (or *brachot*) a day, my Muslim friends hit their knees five times a day in *salat*, and my Vedic friends utter seemingly endless *mantras*. But, alas, most practices still don't specifically address the issue I'm concerned with here, either.

So, then, how are we to regard the deaths of animals from farms, fisheries, fur farms, tanneries, university research labs, medical facilities, vet schools, and so on? Some of you might be thinking, *Oh now, come on. She's gone too far. What, am I supposed to bury them and hold a funeral?* Well played, readers! Alas, even if I wanted to, we can't. The systems regarding the disposal of these animal bodies are multi-stepped, gruesome, and heartbreaking.

The first thing we can do is try to prevent some of the deaths by using fewer animal products. For some people, this means living a vegan lifestyle. Others may favor reducing reliance on animal products through a phased approach like Meatless Mondays, Veganuary, Flexitarian, or Vegan Before 6. And some of your ears might have perked up about that DefaultVeg idea for an upcoming wedding, church potluck, or meditation retreat. Or start by phasing in plant-based meat a couple of days a week.

Those unwilling, unable, or uninterested in changing to compassionate diets could start by committing to animal-free fashion choices such as animal-free leather. It's quite easy these days to select beauty and household products that are not tested on animals or include animal parts in them. (You don't have to identify as a vegan to use vegan face cream!) And all of us could benefit from looking more closely at the label of anything we purchase. Likewise, we should all be reducing single-use plastic which injures animals and is making a freaking mess of our planet. Perhaps, most importantly, we need to get educated on where the products we use come from, and how they may be complicit in the suffering of animals, the planet, and our fellow human beings.

As an added incentive, some recent studies show that treating animals well can lead to us behaving better toward other humans. Promoting the inherent worth of specific animal lives can help us increase our reverence for all lives.[177]

Another practical action we can take is to refuse to turn away from the dying, instead treating them with reverence. Perhaps our raising awareness of animal deaths can help us reconsider the potential meanings of their lives. So, let's look at a few ways spiritually minded and compassionate humans approach these losses.

Memorializing Farmed and Corporate Animal Deaths

In 2011, dual epidemics of foot-and-mouth disease and avian flu pummeled South Korea. Millions of animals were killed—many buried or burned alive because of a lack of euthanasia drugs.[178] Hundreds of South Korean Buddhists responded. Gathering at Joyge Temple, they chanted sutras and bowed reverently to photographs of a pig, cow, and chicken. Candles, fruit, and flowers filled the remainder of the altar. Some monks placed white chrysanthemums there as well, a symbol of grief. The smell of burning mortuary tablets and incense wafted through the air. Gongs clanged and bells were struck. Throughout the day, participants wrote blessings and condolence messages on long white banners, which were strung side by side.[179]

Japan also has a long history of ritually morning animals

owing to Shinto roots combined with Buddhist beliefs. Since the invention of harpoons in the early Edo Period (1603-ish), whaling and mourning whales evolved simultaneously and continue to this day. Mayumi Itoh, author of *The Japanese Culture of Mourning Whales: Whale Graves and Memorial Monuments in Japan,* explains, "The memorial rite for whales began with creating whale graves by burying a part of their bones and erecting gravestones. Then, the Japanese conducted funeral services and mourned their deaths according to the Buddhist precept. Afterward, they performed seasonal and annual memorial services for whales and continued to pray that their souls would rest in peace in Heaven… and to pray that their souls would attain the enlightenment of Buddha."[180] Interestingly, Itoh also notes that the memorial practices have extended beyond whaling communities to include whales who have been beached.[181]

In 2018, the folks at PETA wanted to memorialize 70 crates of lobsters who died when a truck overturned on a Maine highway. But the Department of Transportation denied their request to place a permanent tombstone at the site. PETA's attempt warms my heart, though, as I never bought into my father's declaration as he dropped a live lobster into a pot of scalding water: "Oh, they can't feel it." That practice is illegal now in Switzerland, Norway, New Zealand, Austria, and some cities in Germany and Italy due to anticruelty legislation.[182] (And perhaps soon in the UK, where the British Veterinary Association, Crustacean Compassion, and other welfare groups are advocating for the same, fueled by scientists who suggest that—surprise, surprise—lobsters can indeed feel.)[183]

Over in Wroclaw, Poland, a goose, two pigs, a rabbit,

a rooster, and a goat, all fashioned in heavy bronze, appear permanently stuck in time on a sidewalk where the city's meat market once stood. Created in 1997, the monument stands as a reminder of the animals slaughtered there before the butchering industry was driven outside of town.[184]

And in the US, a solitary bronze cow stands proudly in Sherborn, Massachusetts; her story shared on a plaque beneath her:

> On November 14, 1995, Emily the Cow jumped a 5' gate out of a slaughterhouse in Hopkinton, Massachusetts, and ran for her life. For 40 days, townspeople helped her evade capture and the sure return to the killing floor. Through backyards, state forests, family gardens, in record amounts of snow, Emily was spotted foraging for food, was often seen running with a herd of deer. Making headlines in local newspapers, the story of Emily's plight reached the Rands family, who purchased her from the slaughterhouse. With friends, they brought her to live in sanctuary at the Peace Abbey on Christmas Eve.[185]

Across the country, in Skagway, Alaska, a well-worn bronze plaque is attached to a concrete base in a plaza near the railway station. Initially placed in 1929 by Florence Hartshorn and the Ladies of the Golden North, it honors pack animals who died on the Chilkoot and White Pass Trails in the Klondike's goldfields. The inscription reads, "The dead are speaking. In memory of us 3,000 pack animals that laid our bones on these awful hills during the gold rush of 1897 to 1898. We now thank those listening souls that heard our groans across this stretch of years. We waited but not in vain."[186]

In fact, statues and plaques like these appear all over the world. And not just in parks and along trails, but also outside corporate headquarters, where they acknowledge animals used for "scientific purposes." (It's estimated that humans experiment on about 192 million animals in labs, universities, and research facilities.[187]) I find many of these tributes heartbreaking because they perpetuate the troubling concepts of animals' sacrifice and human gratitude that I unpacked a few pages ago.

For example, a memorial stone outside of the Samsung Biomedical Research Institute in Seoul, Korea, includes a *Prayer for Precious Souls*, which states, "To thankful souls which devoted their previous life for human health, we will do our best to make your devotion more useful and to reduce your sacrifice."[188] As you might expect, I have a lot of issues with the language in this memorial. Just who is thankful? *Devoted* their lives?

A plaque at Merck Research Laboratories in Rahway, New Jersey, states, "In tribute to research animals whose contributions have saved millions of human and animal lives and reduced suffering worldwide. From the animal technicians, supervisors, managers, veterinarians, and research scientists who care for research animals."[189] This, at least, feels a little more truthful. Contributions without consent, of course, but there's no suggestion the animals signed up in some way.

A gigantic bespectacled bronze mouse appears outside the Institute of Cytology and Genetics of the Russian

Academy of Sciences in Akademgorodok, known as Siberia's Silicon Valley. He clutches a double helix and represents the millions of mice killed each year for science.[190] And over on the Black Sea coast in Sokhumi at the Scientific Research Institute of Experimental Pathology and Therapy, there's a massive, frilled baboon statue festooned with a plaque detailing the diseases for which monkeys in the facility were experimented on.[191]

Laika, the first dog to orbit space, also has a memorial. A stray found on the streets of Moscow, she is honored for being sent into space in *Sputnik 2*, with one meal and seven days' worth of oxygen.[192] Sadly, humans have launched many beings into space on one-way trips. No, these beings did not exactly have sacred sendoffs.

Luckily, some do return, including Ham, the first chimp in space, who paved the way for the US's first human astronaut. Sean and I visited Ham last year in front of the International Space Hall of Fame in Alamogordo, New Mexico, where a plaque at his gravesite proudly proclaims, "World's First Astrochimp." To be accurate, not all of Ham is there. NASA notes, "Upon his death, January 17, 1983, Ham's skeleton was retained for ongoing examination by the Armed Forces Institute of Pathology," and his "other remains" were respectfully laid to rest at Alamogordo.[193]

Remembering Invisible Animals

Over the past 100 years, in addition to concerns about the way animals are farmed, the use of animals in medical or scientific research also has been increasingly critiqued. As a result, many researchers have adopted principles developed in the late 1950s, referred to as the Three Rs: *Replacement* suggests that if a method can be used that avoids using animals, it should replace one that does. *Reduction* seeks to minimize the number of animals needed in an experiment. *Refinement* encourages minimizing animal suffering and welfare improvement.[194]

Susan Iliff, a senior research veterinarian at Merck Research Laboratories (Merck & Co.), suggests a fourth "R" is needed to help humans who work with animals in laboratory or research settings: *Remembering*. Iliff states, "One critical and supportive step to assist workers in developing appropriate coping mechanisms is to validate their feelings and the existence of these attachments [to animals]."[195]

Surveying gatherings at various companies around the world, Iliff observes, "Whether of a sacred or secular nature, acknowledgment, memorial, or tribute services and ceremonies provide ways to assist individuals in their coping process. Such venues affirm and validate the existence of an individual's feelings regarding the value and importance of the animals."[196] She also points to the ways in which researchers are acknowledging the costs of research and development, such as the words of an address at the University of Guelph's Center for the Study of Animal Welfare:

> We are causing animals to be born, causing them to live through a variety of unusual experiences, and causing them to die. This is a form of power that cannot be taken lightly. Today is an opportunity to acknowledge the animals' role in what we do. To acknowledge

that without them our research and teaching would be fundamentally altered. To thank the animals seems logically inappropriate because their contribution was taken, not given. Yet we are grateful for, and even dependent upon, their role.… Spend a few moments reflecting upon the things we have talked about here today. And, in your own way, acknowledge what it represents.[197]

It occurs to me that while these words do little to mitigate the animals whose lives were lost, it is a step in the right direction. I appreciate the call for humans to acknowledge suffering. With these words, the university avoids suggesting the animals were devoted to the research, or sacrificed themselves, or consented in any way. No, instead, it clearly states that their contribution was taken. The honesty in these words touches me, and there is an unforgettable wisdom in the final statement: *Acknowledge what this represents.* Within the act of remembering there is also a reminder. When we make invisible losses visible, rather than deny a loss has happened, we bring forth something for reflection. Can remembering help us be more realistic? What if we extended this thought into our before-meal prayers or grace, rather than relying on illogical allusions to noble sacrifice? What if we didn't turn away from the animal costs in our human lives? Instead of being merely grateful or thankful, what if we were honest?

Reflection

BECAUSE EVEN FOR those who have already committed to living a spiritual, or even nonviolent, lifestyle, there is room for reflection and strengthening our commitment to compassion. As much as we each might not want to think about it, we have been complicit in the taking of an animal's life for human purposes—either personally, or, more likely, through a product we purchased, a meal we ate, a piece of clothing we wore, a car that we drove, or a pandemic vaccine we received. Yeah, me included—more than once.

These deaths were likely not acknowledged and instead taken for granted. Because that's the norm in our society. But what if it wasn't?

What if we could acknowledge these losses without sugar-coating them, without trying to make them pleasant or acceptable. Using the University of Guelph's lead, what if we wrote our own statements of acknowledgment.

Here's mine: "I acknowledge that even though I aspire to live a life of nonviolence, I sometimes fall short. My boundless love of cats means other animals will be killed to feed the ones in my home. It also means the mice under my house live with increased risk. When driving, I realize many tiny, winged ones will lose their lives, unable to get out of the way of my windshield. I acknowledge that the COVID-19 vaccine I accepted was created through pain to other beings who were used without their consent, privileging my life over theirs. I am deeply sorrowful about this. Furthermore, I refuse to ignore each of these invisible losses. I commit to being aware of the impact my choices have, choosing those that encourage flourishing and reduce suffering. I acknowledge this is messy work that is often confusing. And so, I commit to seeking out others who will join me in exploring difficult decisions about creating a world where no living being is oppressed or used against their will for any purpose."

Let me be crystal clear: This practice is not intended to depress you. Or to make you feel bad, or guilty, or shamed. Instead, I invite you to approach it as freedom—as liberation from all the reasons and rationales we have carefully constructed. For just a moment, we drop the need to create excuses or defend ourselves to others. Instead, we simply acknowledge *what is* and *what could be.*

Chapter 11

TRYING TO HEAL THE PLANET

*F*OR OVER A decade, Sean and I have spent our wedding anniversary on the island of Tobago, in a small coastal town named Castara. I found the location by accident—or perhaps a divine nudge—during a web search. A die-hard traveler by nature, I was surprised after the first visit that I wanted to return again instead of finding somewhere new for the next anniversary. There was something perfect about this offbeat location, where Sean could bake in the sun and swim through the waves, and I could alternate scuba diving and snorkeling with long stretches of reading on our cool, shaded porch.

Yet, returning year after year to this town, where very little changes, highlighted what was changing in me. On our first visit, I was a pescatarian who delighted in the local cuisine—freshly caught langoustines, sweet plantains, and potatoes soaked in butter. Returning a year or two later—no longer eating beings or butter—I faced some challenges.

You see, Castara is a fishing town. And there was no way to avoid it. In the mornings, the local guys would toss a gigantic net out into the bay. Later in the day, they would gather to pull the net in. Then they'd hoist the huge mahi-mahi and wahoo and snapper onto their shoulders and head to the cooperative building where the fish would be "processed." After swimming around all day with marine life, it pained me to watch this. So, while tourists flocked to watch the live action, I'd sneak into our room to make some cold pasta salad.

Our local friends tolerated my idiosyncrasies—that I no longer ate fish, drank rum, or smoked cigarettes. Occasionally, feeling left out at tropical cocktail hour, I'd proclaim, "I used to do all three! And really well!" Hours later, I'd feel a knot in my stomach from dropping my values so quickly to feel "part of."

Then, one day, when the tide went out, hundreds, if not thousands of tiny, silvery fishes washed up on shore, still alive but beached. I hurried down to the sand and began tossing them one by one back into the retreating surf. Soon, heartbroken, I became aware that there was just no way that I could get them all back into the ocean. I also realized that a lot of people were staring at me. The perfect storm of compassion fatigue and embarrassment washed over me. I was angry, and sad, and confused all at the same time. Here I was in a tropical paradise, yet I was full of anguish knowing that others did not see what I could see—these beings were dying right in front of us while humans sat around sipping fruity drinks. Why wasn't anyone helping me?

And then, about 20 yards down the beach, I saw a little girl—no older than five or six years old—doing the same thing. One by one, she bent down, picked up a small fish by the tail fin, and plopped the sea creature into the water. I smiled. I felt hope.

Embracing Hope

How do we maintain hope when surrounded by so much loss? Many of us have become wary. We are not sure how much more we can take in. Sometimes, it can feel too overwhelming *to know.*

As a result, it can be easy to look for a way out, falling back on the *cycle of nature* excuses. But, as we've explored in this book, humanity is complicit in changing "nature." To suggest that all animal deaths are beyond our ability to change—or beyond our responsibility—is a convenient spiritual bypass. If we want to profess being part of an interconnected, interdependent biosphere, then we have a responsibility to act. We need to try to heal the Earth— not just to sustain our own species, but to sustain all the life we claim to be interconnected with and compassion- ate about.

Whether we can heal the Earth is a question of fierce debate these days. As I polished the final manuscript for this book, the UN's Intergovernmental Panel on Climate Change (IPCC) released its Sixth Assessment Report, in anticipation of the next global climate summit. More than 1,300 pages detailed the findings of over 200 scientists, outlining what the IPCC thinks is in store for us, includ- ing continued retreat of glaciers, hotter oceans, extreme heatwaves, long-term droughts, and severe weather. The impact of these events causes increasingly widespread problems as we struggle to adequately feed ourselves with crops that cannot thrive and to live in communities threatened by coastal erosion, fire, pollution, and other challenges. Moreover, these environmental problems lead to food availability issues, habitat loss, and even extinction for nonhuman animals.

Scientists, environmentalists, educators, politicians, tech giants, consumer goods companies, and religious leaders propose what actions we should take to be environmentally responsible. Some say there's hope. Others say we're doomed and live for today. Many people hold fast to a belief that life here on Earth will be replaced miraculously with something more resplendent. And some humans head out in spaceships looking for new planets to inhabit.

From my point of view healing the planet is necessarily an interspecies activity. Healing goes well beyond ensuring the sustainability of resources for humans and their offspring. When we stop viewing the Earth's many beings as products and instead see them as community members in the more-than-human world, we are more likely to act in ways that help them—and their habitats—flourish.

As we've seen, determining what balance looks like is a complicated endeavor, and yet we have to start somewhere. And so, an animal chaplain's advice is this: Healing Earth starts by repairing all our broken interspecies relationships. Throughout this book, I have proposed ways to do this. First, I suggested that how we talk about and categorize animals undoubtedly affects how we treat them. Then I pulled the curtain back a bit to expose where dominionism, speciesism, and carnism can show up in our thinking. Next, I proposed that addressing these issues is entangled with the racism, ableism, and other troubling *isms* we face—that human and animal issues cannot be disentangled. We've also looked at how our choices impact other beings: who we keep in our homes, how we treat the land we live on, how we drive, how we vacation, what we eat and wear, and what products we buy.

We've also considered the joys of living in an interspecies world. The richness we can experience from relationships with canines, felines, lions, squirrels, and [insert your favorite animal here]. We've seen how we can show boundless love and compassion for animals while they are alive and honor them after they take their last breath.

Along the way, I've left breadcrumbs about some sneaky illusions I think we unknowingly cling to about animal life and death. It's my conviction that by ditching these misunderstandings, we can not only attend to our lingering heartbreaks from animal loss but also encourage all Earthlings and our shared planet to thrive. Our illusions are ideas our ancestors constructed, that we continue to scaffold and patch and mend, even though they are not worth repairing. True healing starts by tearing these misconceptions down, revealing what lies hidden beneath.

Illusion #1: I am not an animal.

To break this illusion is to acknowledge and embrace our animality. We need to stop saying someone is "acting like an animal." And we must watch our language to ensure it is not violent or unkind to other species. We need to stop offering "to be a guinea pig" or "taking the bull by the horns" or criticizing people for being "pig-headed." We must no longer declare, "I don't mean to beat a dead horse, but . . . " or suggest that there is "more than one way to skin a cat" or "kill two birds with one stone." It would also be helpful if we stopped thingifying animals ("I had the juiciest chicken for lunch!" or "I just love leather!"). Because underneath that product, there is—or was—a being. Furthermore, these statements can create deep anguish for people in our communities who have taken a Bodhisattva vow, practice *ahimsa* (nonviolence) as part of their yoga practice, or are ethical vegans. We should stop using the word *dehumanize*, too, since it is built on a foundation that human animals should be treated better than other animals.

Illusion #2: Only humans have spiritual lives.

To break this illusion is to release our claim to human exceptionalism and supremacy. We must engage with other species at a spiritual level. This means including their names and needs in our communal prayers, our religious liturgies, and our personal spiritual practices. We must encourage our religious leaders to address issues of animal exploitation in their sermons, dharma talks, homilies, khutbahs, and derashot. And we need to acknowledge that our animal companions need quiet time by themselves just like we do.

Illusion #3: Wildlife loss is natural and unavoidable.

To break this illusion is to understand that other beings have just as much right to be anywhere as we do. We must stop overdriving our roads. Instead, by slowing down and scanning the roadsides, we give ourselves time to react if another being enters the roadway. Approaching driving as a practice of mindfulness is useful for us too—our vehicles can become a place of quiet respite from the noise of the world where we can focus on doing one thing, driving safely.

We need to think about what we place in "our" yards, planting in ways that can nourish other species—and avoiding practices that put them in danger.

Illusion #4: I can trust that my country has laws that protect the welfare of animals.

To break this illusion is to be active advocates—not just animal lovers. We must educate ourselves on the challenges facing other species and then take action.

Illusion #5: The food I buy is created humanely and sustainably.

To break this illusion is to acknowledge that it probably is not. We must acquiesce to the fact that less than 1 percent of US consumers eat meat from non-factory farms.[198] And that "cage-free" and "free-range" are deceptive terms. And that "organic" and "natural" mean very little when it comes to animal welfare. Ditto for "sustainable." Learn what these terms truly mean and which brands and foods are actually humane. Commit to researching the products and brands you buy. Ask questions and steer clear of any process that treats a living being in a way that you would not want to be treated. Visit farmers to ask them about how they grow the food they sell and how they hire and treat people who work for them. If you are still eating animals, visit the farms and fisheries where they live and ask questions there, too. Commit also to researching the impact of what you eat on the Earth. For example, animal agriculture is a leading source of greenhouse gasses and major cause of air and water pollution.[199] Fully understand where your food comes from and ensure it aligns with your values.

Illusion #6: People who disagree with me are my enemies.

To break this illusion is to accept that we have all been socialized in conflicting ways. We must stop demonizing those who believe different things than we do. Instead, we must approach them with curiosity and figure out what is causing them to support ideas, ideologies, and policies that are violent to others. Once we figure out how someone developed their belief, we may be able to compassionately ask them questions that can broaden their viewpoint. At the same time, their experiences may broaden ours.

In addition, we need to acknowledge that we don't know everything—and, indeed, sometimes we might even be wrong. Well-structured discussions between people with opposing opinions can reveal where each side might be lacking knowledge of the other's challenges, concerns, and needs. Preaching angrily at each other on social media rarely accomplishes much.

Illusion #7: We live on Earth.

To break this illusion is to acknowledge that we are Earth. We need to remember that we are made of star stuff and influenced by tides. That what we eat creates the weather and what we build alters the planet. We must acknowledge that we are part of the planet, not some independent being placed on top of it to use it.

Illusion #8: Change is hard.

To break this illusion is to recognize that change undertaken alone is more difficult than change undertaken with others. We must find mentors who can guide us through the tough places where we are stuck. Groups who are interested in the causes we are interested in. A spiritual community that supports our values and guides us in practices that connect us to something greater than ourselves. Friends who can ground us when we're rageful or sobbing.

And wild spaces where we can sit silently, taking in the sights, sounds, and smells of the planet we are trying so desperately to help heal.

LIVING BEYOND OUR LIVES

*O*NE DAY EACH of our bodies will be called a *corpse.* And people will make decisions about what to do with it. They will wonder where we have gone. They will miss us and grieve. And in the midst of that, they will need to wrap up our worldly lives.

When my father died, it happened quickly and unexpectedly over six excruciating weeks. He was merely 65 when cancer exploded through his organs. It was the most difficult thing I have ever been through. Unless you count the months following his death. Because, along with my grief, confusion, and anger, there were bills to pay and critical paperwork to find. There were funeral plans to make and endless phone calls to answer. For over a year, there were so many financial, medical, and legal tasks that my sister and I felt like we had second jobs. And there was my mother to care for as she lost her lifelong partner.

I'll be the first to admit my father was amazing at supporting other people. The stories people shared with me at his funeral only proved what I had known all my life:

my father cared deeply and gave generously. And yet, I'd be remiss not to mention that he lacked three essential skills—maintaining cars, paying his quarterly estimated taxes on time, and organizing his paperwork in a logical way that made sense to any of us. It took months to find his will among the stacks and stacks of papers that filled his home office and even longer to sort out his estate.

As a result of that experience, when Sean and I got married, I started a binder explaining everything anyone would need to do if I died—every account number, phone number, and password. I shopped for long-term care insurance and went to Medicare seminars even though I was nowhere near retirement age. I studied actuarial charts and researched the lifetime costs of various diseases. These actions—which may seem a bit overly proactive for someone in their late 30s—were driven by a desire to make my eventual death easier on those I left behind. Then, while attending seminary, I wrote a detailed plan for my funeral.

And that is how, on one vacation, Sean was subjected to a weeklong conversation about how and where we should be buried. "Do you want to be shot into space, become a reef, or have our ashes covertly scattered some-where amazing?" I asked him. As often happens with me, once I have an exciting idea, I am swept away researching myself into a hypermanic state, downloading oodles of links and documents and photos. When passionate about something, I can easily overwhelm people. "Can't we just simply be buried in the ground?" Sean asked. And that is how—after considering ocean burial, mummification, cryonics, and myriad other options—we decided on a simple green burial at our local cemetery. No embalming fluid or coffin to keep us from becoming Earth. No high-temperature flames emitting carbon dioxide into the air. No toxic rocket fuel to launch us into orbit. For a bit of flair, we agreed that I would purchase two burial shrouds at a future date, on which he would paint meaningful symbols with nontoxic paint, and then we would store them in the attic until they were needed.

Thus, satisfied with this earth-friendly option and dreaming of all critters who might munch the vegetation on top of my grave, I got back to writing my kickass funeral service, complete with my niece belting out "Defying Gravity" from *Wicked*, a meditation on an acoustic version of Alanis Morrissette's *Ironic,* a reading from Bible and then one from *The Tao of the Force* followed by the Mourner's Kaddish, wrapping up with the Serenity Prayer. As for Sean's funeral, he reflected, "Whatever you think. I'll be dead."

In the years since then, we have made other decisions about our end days. Most importantly, we have decided that we, above all, want our deaths to sustain life. Choosing green burial—to become part of the biotic community *within* the Earth—was just the first step. Next, we decided while we were still living, we would continue to live in ways that minimize the death of other beings. The third decision was making sure our wills included planned giving, which would donate part of what remained in our savings and retirement accounts at our death to lifesaving actions for the Earth and its many beings. Of course, we also let Sean's son and my sister know where to find the binder with our detailed instructions. And we decided who would take care of whatever companion animals might be living with us at the time of our death to ensure they would not be surrendered to a shelter.

As an act of forward-looking compassion to all we love, we planned our own sacred sendoffs.

May my presence be a blessing to all creatures.

Blessed furriness walking on four legs,
may you be sustained and flourish.
Blessed feathered of the skies,
may you be sustained and flourish.
Blessed finned beings of the waters,
may you be sustained and flourish.
Blessed leafed ones rooted in the Earth,
may you be sustained and flourish.

Glory be to the Forests, and to the Deserts,
and to the Holy Seas.
As it was in the beginning,
is now, and ever shall be.

May I live in connection to the everlasting cycle of life,
And when this body no longer can sustain me,

May I be blessed with a sacred sendoff.

ACKNOWLEDGMENTS

First and foremost, this work was possible through the ongoing support of my husband, Sean Bowen, who is endlessly subjected to interspecies musings and has endured many impromptu announcements that his wife needed to go hermit to *finish the unfinishable book.*

I am once again grateful to journey with the creative souls at Monkfish Book Publishing Company: publisher Paul Cohen for his uncanny ability to swoop in with encouragement when I'm burned-out, editor Susan Piperato for her gentle guidance, designer Colin Rolfe for his creative collaboration, and proofreader Dory Mayo for her exacting finish on the work. Praise also to Diane Walters for early editing support, including entertaining entirely too many conversations with me about my love of hyphens and sassy punctuation.

I am deeply indebted to Rev. Diane Berke and Rev. eileen fisher of One Spirit Interfaith Seminary for their ongoing reassurance that my love for Rodentia—as well as concern for flattened fauna, oppressed Bovinae, and myriad other beings—is indeed a sacred calling. Likewise, a debt of gratitude goes to Ken Stone and Cody J. Sanders, whose work at Chicago Theological Seminary has stretched my thinking on animality and deathways.

Thankfully, I am supported by many human animals including Barbara Becker, Elizabeth Friend-Ennis, Marshall Hammer, Susan Loving, Mac Buff, Julie Britton, Stephanie Niemala, and Zulma Gonzalez, who provided moments of light-heartedness that were essential for sustaining this often-heart-breaking endeavor.

Thanks also to William Melton for insisting this world needed a church-ish organization for animal advocates and invited me to help form it. Gratitude to Victoria Moran for modeling the route to where equanimity and advocacy meet. And to Erika Allison for her contagious joy. Please come worship with us. Details at compassionconsortium.org.

Finally, I would be remiss not to mention the invaluable contributions of every squirrel I've ever known, my feline companions, Deacon and Buba-ji, and the many nameless creatures appearing in the preceding pages. Ultimately, they inspired this work, which is merely recorded by my human hands.

BIBLIOGRAPHY

Abram, David. *The Spell of the Sensuous: Perception and Language in a More-than-human World.* 20th ed. New York: Vintage Books, a division of Penguin Random House, 2017.

American Battlefield Trust. "The Cost of War: Killed, Wounded, Captured, and Missing." Civil War Casualties, August 19, 2021. battlefields.org/learn/articles/civil-war-casualties.

American Humane. "2014 Humane HeartlandTM Farm Animal Welfare Survey," August 28, 2014. americanhumane.org/publication/2014-humane-heartland-farm-animal-welfare-survey.

American Society for the Prevention of Cruelty to Animals. "Species Suitable to Be Companion Animals." Policies and Positions. aspca.org/about-us/aspca-policy-and-position-statements/species-suitable-be-companion-animals.

Amiot, Catherine E., and Brock Bastian. "Toward a Psychology of Human–Animal Relations." *Psychological Bulletin* 141, no. 1 (January 2015): 6–47. doi.org/10.1037/a0038147.

Animal Humane Society. "The Five Freedoms for Animals." animalhumanesociety.org/health/five-freedoms-animals.

Animal Interfaith Alliance. "Faiths Working Together for Animals." 2021. animal-interfaith-alliance.com.

Anthis, Jacy Reese. "Survey of US Attitudes toward Animal Farming and Animal-Free Food." Sentience Institute. November 20, 2017.

Anthis, Jacy Reese. *The End of Animal Farming: How Scientists, Entrepreneurs, and Activists Are Building an Animal-free Food System*. Boston: Beacon Press, 2019.

Anthis, Jacy Reese. "US Factory Farming Estimates: Table." Sentience Institute. April 11, 2019. sentienceinstitute.org/us-factory-farming-estimates.

Associated Press. "Dead Whale Brings Majestic Moments, Big Problems for Beach." *Oroville Mercury-Register*, April 27, 2016. orovillemr.com/2016/04/27/dead-whale-brings-majestic-moments-big-problems-for-beach.

Associated Press Archive. "Buddhist Ritual for Cows and Pigs Culled with Foot-and-Mouth Disease." YouTube. Accessed July 30, 2015. youtube.com/watch?v=4M-QFoLbtuw.

Atlas Obscura. "Monument in Honor of the Slaughtered Animals." Wrocław, Poland. atlasobscura.com/places/monument-in-honor-of-the-slaughtered-animals.

Bailey, Emily. "Making Sense of Religion and Food." *Bulletin for the Study of Religion* 46, no. 2 (July 4, 2017): 18–24. doi.org/10.1558/bsor.32163.

Banfield Pet Hospital. "New Survey Reveals Effects Stay-at-Home Order May Have on Pets and Their Owners." *Cision: PR Newswire*. May 26, 2020. prnewswire.com/news-releases/new-survey-reveals-effects-stay-at-home-order-may-have-on-pets-and-their-owners-301064494.html.

Bar-On, Yinon M., Rob Phillips, and Ron Milo. "The biomass

distribution on Earth." *Proceedings of the National Academy of Sciences* 115, no. 25 (2018): 6506–6511.

Barnett, Lindsay. "South Korea Culls Animals on Huge Scale in Response to Foot-and-Mouth Disease, Avian Flu Outbreaks." *Los Angeles Times*, January 20, 2011. latimesblogs.latimes.com/unleashed/2011/01/south-korea-foot-mouth-disease-buries-pigs-alive.html.

Bartal, Inbal Ben-Ami, Jean Decety, and Peggy Mason. "Empathy and Pro-Social Behavior in Rats." *Science* 334, no. 6061 (2011): 1427–1430.

Bartram, D. J., and D. S. Baldwin. "Veterinary Surgeons and Suicide: A Structured Review of Possible Influences on Increased Risk." *Veterinary Record* 166, no. 13 (March 27, 2010): 388–97. doi.org/10.1136/vr.b4794.

Bates, Mary. "Prehistoric Puppy May Be Earliest Evidence of Pet-Human Bonding." *National Geographic.* February 26, 2018. nationalgeographic.com/news/2018/02/ancient-pet-puppy-oberkassel-stone-age-dog.

Becker, Ernest. *The Denial of Death.* New York: Free Press, 1975.

Bever, Lindsey. "Another Country Bans Boiling Live Lobsters as Scientists Debate Whether They Feel Pain." *Chicago Tribune*, January 13, 2018. chicagotribune.com/news/environment/ct-boiling-live-lobster-ban-20180113-story.html.

Bowen, Sarah, and Richard Murdoch. *Void If Detached: Seeking Modern Spirituality through My Father's Old Sermons.* Rhinebeck, NY: Teras Publishing, 2016.

Brooks Pribac, Teya. *Enter the Animal: Cross-Species Perspectives on Grief and Spirituality.* Sydney: Sydney University Press, 2021.

Chur-Hansen, Anna. "Cremation Services upon the Death of a Companion Animal: Views of Service Providers and Service Users." *Society and Animals 19*, no. 3 (2011): 248–60. doi. org/10.1163/156853011X578910.

Chur-Hansen, Anna. "Grief and Bereavement Issues and the Loss of a Companion Animal: People Living with a Companion Animal, Owners of Livestock, and Animal Support Workers." *Clinical Psychologist 14*, no. 1 (March 2010): 14–21. doi.org/10.1080/13284201003662800.

Cincinnati Zoo & Botanical Garden. "Passenger Pigeon Memorial: The Story of Martha." cincinnatizoo.org/plan-your-visit/exhibits/passenger-pigeon-memorial.

Clough, David L., Margaret B. Adam, David Grumett, and Siobhan Mullan. *The Christian Ethics of Farmed Animal Welfare: A Policy Framework for Churches and Christian Organizations*. CEFAW, 2020. www1.chester.ac.uk/christian-ethics-farmed-animal-welfare/cefaw-policy-framework.

Collier, Ivy D. "More than a Bag of Bones: A History of Animal Burials." In *Mourning Animals: Rituals and Practices Surrounding Animal Death*, edited by Margo DeMello. East Lansing, MI: Michigan State University Press, 2016, 3–10.

Colvin, Christina M. "Freeze-Dried Fido: The Uncanny Aesthetics of Modern Taxidermy." In *Mourning Animals: Rituals and Practices Surrounding Animal Death*, edited by Margo DeMello. East Lansing, MI: Michigan State University Press, 2016, 65–71.

Connor, Richard, and Kenneth S. Norris. "Are Dolphins Reciprocal Altruists?" *The American Naturalist* 119, no. 3. journals.uchicago.edu/doi/10.1086/283915.

Connor, Steven. "End of the Furry Tale: The Life and Death of Knut." *Independent*. March 21, 2011. independent.co.uk/

climate-change/news/end-of-the-furry-tale-the-life-and-death-of-knut-2247762.html.

Crimston, Charlie R., Paul G. Bain, Matthew J. Hornsey, and Brock Bastian. "Moral Expansiveness: Examining Variability in the Extension of the Moral World." *Journal of Personality and Social Psychology* 111, no. 4 (October 2016): 636–53. doi.org/10.1037/pspp0000086.

Cronin, J. Keri. *Art for Animals: Visual Culture and Animal Advocacy, 1870–1914.* University Park, PA: Penn State University Press, 2018.

Cruelty Free International. "Facts and Figures on Animal Testing." https://www.crueltyfreeinternational.org/why-we-do-it/facts-and-figures-animal-testing.

Crustation Compassion. "Campaigning for the Humane Treatment of Crabs, Lobsters and Other Decapod Crustaceans in the UK." The Voice Project. crustaceancompassion.org.uk.

Cryonics. "Pet Cryopreservation." cryonics.org/resources/pet-cryopreservation.

Daily News. "War Dog Given Hero's Funeral" *Hartsdale Pet Cemetery and Crematory.* February 21, 2001. hartsdalepetcrematory.com/news/war-dog-given-heros-funeral.

Davies, Douglas James. *Death, Ritual, and Belief: The Rhetoric of Funerary Rites.* 3rd ed. London: Bloomsbury Academic, 2017.

Dayer, Ashley A., Kent H. Redford, Karl J. Campbell, Christopher R. Dickman, Rebecca S. Epanchin-Niell, Edwin D. Grosholz, David E. Hallac, Elaine F. Leslie, Leslie A. Richardson, and Mark W. Schwartz. "The Unaddressed Threat of Invasive Animals in U.S. National Parks." *Biological Invasions 22*, no. 2 (2020): 177–88. doi.org/10.1007/s10530-019-02128-0.

de Jong, Gigi. "Treacherous Footing: When 122 Deer Plunge off an Icy Sierra Nevada Cliff, People Ask How Something like This Could Happen." *Outdoor California* 80, no. 1 (January/February 2019): 36–39.

de Waal, Frans. *Are We Smart Enough to Know How Smart Animals Are?* New York: W.W. Norton & Company, 2017.

Democrat and Chronicle, "Seneca Park Zoo Recycles Roadkill." democratandchronicle.com/story/news/2014/08/20/seneca-park-zoo-lions-deer-roadkill/14356667.

DeMello, Margo. *Animals and Society: An Introduction to Human-Animal Studies.* New York: Columbia University Press, 2012.

Dharma Voices for Animals. "Right Eating: What the Buddha Taught." Last modified July 9, 2014. dharmavoicesforanimals.org/eating.

Dosa, David M. "A Day in the Life of Oscar the Cat." *New England Journal of Medicine* 357, no. 4 (July 26, 2007): 328–29. doi.org/10.1056/NEJMp078108.

El Paso Morning Times. "Last Passenger Pigeon Dies." September 14, 1914. https://texashistory.unt.edu/ark:/67531/metapth197161/m1/6/.

George, Alice. "The Sad, Sad Story of Laika, the Space Dog, and Her One-Way Trip into Orbit." *Smithsonian Magazine.* April 11, 2018. smithsonianmag.com/smithsonian-institution/sad-story-laika-space-dog-and-her-one-way-trip-orbit-1-180968728.

Gershon, Livia. "A Horse's-Eye View of the Civil War." *JSTOR.* April 12, 2019. daily.jstor.org/a-horses-eye-view-of-the-civil-war.

Geyer, Georgie Anne. *When Cats Reigned like Kings: On the Trail of the Sacred Cats.* Kansas City: Andrews McMeel Pub., 2004.

Gibbard, M. Daniel. "Taxidermy Undergoes an Extreme

Makeover." *Chicago Tribune*, March 18, 2006. chicagotribune. com/news/ct-xpm-2006-03-18-0603180240-story.html.

Goldman, Jason G. "Death Rituals in the Animal Kingdom." *BBC*. September 18, 2012. bbc.com/future/article/20120919-respect-the-dead.

Goodall, Jane, and Phillip L. Berman. *Reason for Hope: A Spiritual Journey*. New ed. New York: Warner, 2005.

Gray, Tara. "A Brief History of Animals in Space." *National Aeronautics and Space Administration (NASA)*. 1998. Published August 2, 2004. history.nasa.gov/animals.html.

Green Renaissance. "Highway Memorial." *Vimeo*. August 20, 2012. vimeo.com/47859216.

Greene, Alexander M. "Speaking with an Upside-Down Tongue: Reflections on Human-Elephant Multispecies Culture in Northern Thailand." *Gajah* 53 (2021): 4–19. asesg.org/PDFfiles/2021/53-04-Greene.pdf.

Greene, Eric. "Interview by the Author." Zoom. April 14, 2020.

Grundhauser, Eric. "The Brief, Bright Life of New Zealand's Beloved Celebrity Dolphin." Atlas Obscura. August 22, 2017. atlasobscura.com/articles/opo-friendly-dolphin-new-zealand-opononi.

Hall, Christopher. "Bereavement Theory: Recent Developments in Our Understanding of Grief and Bereavement." *Bereavement Care* 33, no. 1 (May 9, 2014): 7–14. doi.org/10. 1080/02682621.2014.902610.

Handwerk, Brian. "National Zoo Deaths: 'Circle of Life' or Animal Care Concerns?" *National Geographic*. December 17, 2013. nationalgeographic.com/news/2013/12/131217-science-zoo-death-smithsonian-gazelle-hog-zebra-kudu-przewalski.

Hannon, Elliot. "Vanishing Vultures A Grave Matter For India's Parsis." *NPR*. September 5, 2012. npr.org/

2012/09/05/160401322/vanishing-vultures-a-grave-matter-for-indias-parsis.

Hanson, Hilary. "Cat Interrupts Meteorologist Working From Home And Wins A New Job." *Huffpost.* April 18, 2020. https://www.huffpost.com/entry/cat-meteorologist-coronavirus_n_5e938770c5b6d97d91ef428e.

Hardy Vincent, Carol, Carla N. Argueta, and Laura A. Hanson. *Federal Land Ownership: Overview and Data. CRS Report for Congress,* 2017, updated 2021. PDF. fas.org/sgp/crs/misc/R42346.pdf.

Hare, Brian, and Suzy Kwetuenda. "Bonobos voluntarily share their own food with others." *Current Biology 20,* no. 5 (2010): R230–R231.

Harrison, Peter. "Descartes on Animals." *The Philosophical Quarterly (1950–)* 42, no. 167 (1992): 219–227.

Harrod, James B. "A Trans-Species Definition of Religion." *Journal for the Study of Religion, Nature, and Culture* 5, no. 3 (2011). doi.org/10.1558/jsrnc.v5i3.327.

Harrod, James B. "The Case for Chimpanzee Religion." *Journal for the Study of Religion, Nature, and Culture* 8, no. 1 (2014). dx.doi.org/10.1558/jsrnc.v8i1.8.

Hartsdale Pet Cemetery and Crematoria. "War Dog Memorial." *Hartsdale Pet Crematory, Inc.* hartsdalepetcrematory.com/about-us/war-dog-memorial.

Heller, Bruce [Developed by]. *Gotham.* Warner Bros. Television. Aired on FOX, September 22, 2014.

HHR. "Devotion of the Squirrel." *Hindu Human Rights.* June 9, 2013. hinduhumanrights.info/devotion-of-the-squirrel.

Ikram, Salima. *Divine Creatures: Animal Mummies in Ancient Egypt.* Cairo, Egypt: American University in Cairo Press, 2015.

Iliff, Susan A. "An Additional 'R': Remembering the Animals." *ILAR Journal* 43, no. 1 (January 1, 2002): 38–47. doi.org/10.1093/ilar.43.1.38.

Interfaith Vegan Coalition. "Advocacy Kits." In Defense of Animals. idausa.org/campaign/sustainable-activism/interfaith-vegan-coalition/advocacy-kits.

Interfaith Vegan Coalition. "Coalition Members." In Defense of Animals. idausa.org/campaign/sustainable-activism/interfaith-vegan-coalition/coalition-members.

Itoh, Mayumi. *The Japanese Culture of Mourning Whales: Whale Graves and Memorial Monuments in Japan*. Singapore: Palgrave Macmillan, 2018.

Jainism Global Resource Center. "The Compassion of the Elephant." jainworld.com/education/jain-education-material/beginner-level/the-compassion-of-the-elephant.

Joy, Melanie. *Why We Love Dogs, Eat Pigs and Wear Cows: An Introduction to Carnism*. 10th ed. Newburyport: Red Wheel, 2020.

Keiper, Caitrin. "Do Elephants Have Souls?" *The New Atlantis: A Journal of Technology & Society*. (Winter/Spring 2013). thenewatlantis.com/publications/do-elephants-have-souls.

Kemmerer, Lisa A. "Verbal Activism: 'Anymal.'" *Society and Animals* 14, no. 1 (February 2006): 9–14. brill.com/view/journals/soan/14/1/article-p9_3.xml.

Kemp, Hellen R., Nicky Jacobs, and Sandra Stewart. "The Lived Experience of Companion-animal Loss: A Systematic Review of Qualitative Studies." *Anthrozoös* 29, no. 4 (November 22, 2016): 533–57. doi.org/10.1080/08927936.2016.1228772.

Kimmerer, Robin Wall. *Braiding Sweetgrass*. Minneapolis: Milkweed Editions, 2015.

King, Ursula. "*Interfaith Spirituality or Interspirituality? A New Phenomenon in a Postmodern World.*" In *Religious Pluralism and the Modern World*, 107–120. London: Palgrave Macmillan, 2012.

Kiryu City. "Animal Memorial Service." Kiryugaoka Zoo. Last modified October 17, 2019. city.kiryu.lg.jp.e.wt.hp.transer. com/zoo/yomoyama/1015545/1015945.html

Klass, Dennis, and Edith Steffen. *Continuing Bonds in Bereavement: New Directions for Research and Practice.* New York: Routledge, 2017.

Knutson, Roger M. *Flattened Fauna: A Field Guide to Common Animals of Roads, Streets, and Highways*, rev. ed. Berkeley: Ten Speed Press, 2006.

Kolb, Elisabeth. "Composting Roadkilled Deer." *Public Roads* 70, no.1 US Government Printing Office (2006).

Korea Bizwire. "Animal Memorial Ceremony Held at Seoul Grand Park Zoo." Accessed October 29, 2020. koreabizwire. com/animal-memorial-ceremony-held-at-seoul-grand-park-zoo/173237.

Koziel, Jacek A., Heekwon Ahn, Thomas D. Glanville, Timothy S. Frana, J. Hans van Leeuwen, and Lam T. Nguyen. "Lab-Scale Evaluation of Aerated Burial Concept for Treatment and Emergency Disposal of Infectious Animal Carcasses." *Waste Management*, no. 76 (June 2018): 715–26. pubmed. ncbi.nlm.nih.gov/29548829.

LaPriore, Danny. "Greenburgh Police Lay K-9 Officer 'Patriot' To Rest In Hartsdale." *Greenburgh Daily Voice.* October 29, 2013. dailyvoice.com/new-york/greenburgh/news/greenburgh-police-lay-k-9-officer-patriot-to-rest-in-hartsdale/486789.

Larrivee, Denis, and Luis Echarte. "Contemplative Meditation and Neuroscience: Prospects for Mental Health." *Journal of Religion and Health* 57, no. 3 (August 17, 2017): 960–78. doi. org/10.1007/s10943-017-0475-0.

Lee, Laura, and Martyn Lee. *Absent Friend: Coping with the Loss of a Treasured Pet.* Dorking, Surrey: Ringpress, 2002.

Levinson, Lisa. "Interview with the Author." Email. May 17, 2021.

Little, Becky. "The Environmental Toll of Cremating the Dead." *National Geographic.* Published November 5, 2019. nationalgeographic.com/science/2019/11/is-cremation-environmentally-friendly-heres-the-science.

Manokara, Kunalan, Albert Lee, Shanmukh V. Kamble, and Eva G. Krumhuber. "Mind Your Meat: Religious Differences in the Social Perception of Animals." *International Journal of Psychology* 56, no. 3 (September 30, 2020): 466–477. doi. org/10.1002/ijop.12717.

Marris, Emma. "Modern Zoos Are Not Worth the Moral Cost," *New York Times,* June 11, 2021.

Marris, Emma. *Wild Souls: How Animals Can Thrive in a Human-Made World.* London: Bloomsbury, 2021.

Martin, Ed. "Interview by the Author." Zoom. March 18, 2020.

Mascarelli, Amanda. "Dead Whales Make for an Underwater Feast." *Audubon,* November/December 2009. audubon.org/magazine/november-december-2009/dead-whales-make-underwater-feast.

McHugo, Gillian P., Michael J. Dover, and David E. MacHugh. "Unlocking the Origins and Biology of Domestic Animals Using Ancient DNA and Paleogenomics." *BMC Biology* 17, no. 1 (December 2019). doi.org/10.1186/s12915-019-0724-7.

Muller, Joy. "Interview by the Author." Email. Nov 27, 2020.

Monsó, Susana. "How to Tell If Animals Can Understand Death." *Erkenntnis*, December 13, 2019: 1–20. doi. org/10.1007/s10670-019-00187-2.

Morgan, Richard. *Altered Carbon*. New York: Del Rey, 2018.

Morley, Christine, and Jan Fook. "The Importance of Pet Loss and Some Implications for Services." *Mortality* 10, no. 2 (May 2005): 127–43. doi.org/10.1080/1357627041233132 9849.

Moss, Cynthia. *Elephant Memories: Thirteen Years in the Life of an Elephant Family*. Chicago: University of Chicago Press, 2000.

National Highway Traffic Safety Association. "2020 Fatality Data Show Increased Traffic Fatalities During Pandemic." June 3, 2021. nhtsa.gov/press-releases/2020-fatality-data-show-increased-traffic-fatalities-during-pandemic.

New York State. "Pet Cremated Remains FAQ's." *Department of State: Division of Cemeteries*. dos.ny.gov/pet-cremated-remains-frequently-asked-questions.

North American Nature Photography Association, "Truth in Captioning." nanpa.org/tag/truth-in-captioning.

O'Connor, Terry. *Animals as Neighbors: The Past and Present of Commensal Species*. East Lansing:, MI Michigan State University Press, 2013.

Office of the Federal Register (US) 2017. Code of Federal Regulations Title 36 - *Parks, Forests, And Public Property*: revised as of ... July 1, 2017. Lanham, MD: Bernan Press.

Panko, Ben. "This Russian Monument Honors the Humble Lab Mouse," Smithsonian, August 21, 2017, smithsonianmag. com/smart-news/russian-statue-honoring-laboratory-mice-gains-renewed-popularity-180964570.

Patrick, Robert F. "Adoptions of Military Dogs Begins, But Not in Time to Save Robby." Capital News Service. April

27, 2001. cnsmaryland.org/2001/04/27/adoptions-of-military-dogs-begins-but-not-in-time-to-save-robby.

Peaceful Pets Aquamation. "A Closer Look: The Environmental Impact of Pet Cremation vs. Pet Aquamation." peacefulpetsaquamation.com/a-closer-look-the-environmental-impacts-of-pet-cremation-vs-pet-aquamation.

Pearce, Fred. *New Wild: Why Invasive Species Will Be Nature's Salvation.* Boston: Beacon Press, 2016.

Persson, Kirsten, Felicitas Selter, Gerald Neitzke, and Peter Kunzmann. "Philosophy of a 'Good Death' in Small Animals and Consequences for Euthanasia in Animal Law and Veterinary Practice." *Animals* 10, no. 1 (January 13, 2020): 124. doi.org/10.3390/ani10010124.

Pet Food Industry. "Pet Ownership Internationally." petfoodindustry.com/articles/5845-infographic-most-of-world-owns-pets-dogs-are-tops.

PETA. "Animal Rights Uncompromised: 'Pets.'" peta.org/about-peta/why-peta/pets.

PETA. "Dogs in Laboratories." peta.org/issues/animals-used-for-experimentation/dogs-laboratories.

PETA. "Experiments on Animals: Overview." peta.org/issues/animals-used-for-experimentation/animals-used-experimentation-factsheets/animal-experiments-overview.

Pickrell, John. "Oldest Known Pet Cat? 9,500-Year-Old Burial Found on Cyprus." *National Geographic.* April 8, 2004. nationalgeographic.com/animals/2004/04/oldest-known-pet-cat-9500-year-old-burial-found-on-cyprus.

Pierotti, Raymond. "Spite and Altruism in Gulls." *The American Naturalist* 115, no. 2 (February 1980): 290–300. jstor.org/stable/2460600.

Platt, Belinda, Keith Hawton, Sue Simkin, and Richard J.

Mellanby. "Suicidal Behaviour and Psychosocial Problems in Veterinary Surgeons: A Systematic Review." *Social Psychiatry and Psychiatric Epidemiology* 47, no. 2 (Published December 23, 2010): 223–40. doi.org/10.1007/s00127-010-0328-6.

Pflaum Publishing Group. *The Golden Rule Poster.* Table/Poster #5003. n.d. Dayton, OH. pflaum.com/preview/goldrule/goldrule.pdf.

Preston, Michael, Larry Halverson, and Gayle Hesse. "Mitigation Efforts to Reduce Mammal Mortality on Roadways in Kootenay National Park, British Columbia." *Wildlife Afield* 3, no. 1 (June 2006 Supplement): 28–38. wildlifecollisions.ca/docs/B9DBD18130AE20D2.pdf

Pullan, Tessa. *Civil War Horse.* United States Calvary Museum. Historical and Archaeological Society of Fort Riley, 1996. fortrileyhistoricalsociety.org/us-cavalry-museum.html.

Rancher Advocacy Program. "RAP 101." rancheradvocacy.org/rap-101.

Rao, Sailesh. "Animal Agriculture Position Paper." Climate Healers. November 2019. https://climatehealers.org/the-science/animal-agriculture-position-paper.

Rault, Jean-Loup. "Be kind to others: Prosocial behaviours and their implications for animal welfare." *Applied Animal Behaviour Science* 210 (2019): 113–123. doi.org/10.1016/j.applanim.2018.10.015.

Recompose. "Death-Care: Pricing." recompose.life/death-care/#pricing.

Reich, Susan, and David Walker. "Wildlife Photographers Debate Controversial New Practices." *Photo District News* 18, no. 7 (July 1998): 28.

Rémillard, Liam W. and Michael P. Meehan, David F. Kelton & Jason B. Coe (2017). "Exploring the Grief Experience

Among Callers to a Pet Loss Support Hotline, *Anthrozoös*, 30, 1:149-161, doi.org/10.1080/08927936.2017.1270600.

Ritchie, Hannah. "Livestock Outweighs Wild Mammals and Birds Ten-Fold." *Our World in Data*. April 24, 2019. ourworldindata.org/life-on-earth.

Roberts, Holly. *Vegetarian Christian Saints: Mystics, Ascetics and Monks*. San Francisco: Anjeli Press, 2004.

Rooted. "About." Rooted, LLC. rootedpet.com/about.

Russell, William Moy Stratton, and Rex Leonard Burch. *The Principles of Humane Experimental Technique*. Methuen, 1959. Special ed. Wheathampstead: Universities Federation for Animal Welfare, 1999. HTML file. caat.jhsph.edu/principles/the-principles-of-humane-experimental-technique.

Seiler, Andreas, and J. O. Helldin. "Mortality in Wildlife Due to Transportation." In *The Ecology of Transportation: Managing Mobility for the Environment*, 165–189. Dordrecht, Netherlands: Springer Netherlands, 2006.

Sellner, Edward Cletus. *Celtic Saints and Animal Stories: A Spiritual Kinship*. New York: Paulist Press, 2020.

Shufeldt. R. W. "Anatomical and Other Notes on the Passenger Pigeon (Ectopistes Migratorius) Lately Living in the Cincinnati Zoological Gardens." *The Auk* 32, no. 1 (January 1915): 29–41. Published by The American Oritithologists' Union.

Silva, Aline. "Interview by the Author." Zoom. September 23, 2020.

Sivewright, Joe, and Nina Leigh Kruger. "Winning in PetCare: Pet Population." Infographic. *Nestlé Purina*. May 7, 2019. Presentation. nestle.com/sites/default/files/asset-library/documents/library/presentations/investors_events/investor-seminar-2019/petcare.pdf.

Smithsonian. "Martha, the Last Passenger Pigeon." National Museum of Natural History. naturalhistory.si.edu/research/vertebrate-zoology/birds/collections-overview/martha-last-passenger-pigeon.

Solovyov, Dimitry. "Georgia's Lab Apes Languish in Post-Soviet Limbo." Reuters. July 28, 2008. reuters.com/article/us-georgia-monkeys/georgias-lab-apes-languish-in-post-soviet-limbo-idUKL1655341120080729.

Springfield News-Leader, "The Rules of Roadkill." news-leader.com/story/news/local/ozarks/2017/11/08/rules-roadkill/844795001.

Spitzer, Leo. "On the Etymology of Pet." *Language* 26, no. 4 (1950): 533–538. doi.org/10.2307/410403.

Stack, Liam. "How Do You Move a 70,000-Pound (Dead) Whale?" *New York Times*, April 28, 2016. nytimes.com/2016/04/29/us/dead-whale-california-beach.html.

Stahler, Charles. "How Many People Are Vegan? How Many Eat Vegan When Eating Out? Asks the Vegetarian Resource Group." *The Vegetarian Resource Group*. Last modified March 2019. vrg.org/nutshell/Polls/2019_adults_veg.htm.

Staunton Transportation Company: J. B. Staunton. "Transportation of the Dead." H.J. Stahle, printer, "Compiler" Office, Gettysburg, Pa., 1863. *The Library Company of Philadelphia*, 2020. digital.librarycompany.org/islandora/object/Islandora%3A6961.

Stone, Jasmine. "N2 Highway Memorial — 312 Dead Rhinos." *2 Oceans Vibe News*, August 2012. 2oceansvibe.com/2012/08/21/n2-highway-memorial-312-dead-rhinos-video.

Swan, G.E., R. Cuthbert, M. Quevedo, et al. (June 2006). "Diclofenac Effect." *Biology Letters* 2, no. 2: 279–82. doi:10.1098/rsbl.2005.0425.

Summum. "Modern Mummification and Transference." 2016. summum.org/overview.shtml.

Tacoma News Tribune. "Dining on Roadkill: Washington Residents Gather 1,600 Deer, Elk in Law's First Year." thenewstribune.com/news/local/article163842588.html.

Taylor, Sunaura. *Beasts of Burden: Animal and Disability Liberation.* New York: New Press, 2017.

Teasdale, Wayne. *The Mystic Heart: Discovering a Universal Spirituality in the World's Religions.* Novato, CA: New World Library, 2001.

"Terms of Discourse." *Journal of Animal Ethics* 1, no. 1 (2011): Vii–Ix. doi:10.5406/janimalethics.1.1.vii.

The Local de. "Knut's Real Fur Used for New Museum Statue." thelocal.de/20130212/47923#.USH3gasiGW9.

Tatanka: Story of the Bison. "Kevin Costner Invites You to Visit Tatanka." storyofthebison.com/

Tkatch, Rifky, Lizi Wu, Stephanie MacLeod, Rachel Ungar, Laurie Albright, Daniel Russell, James Murphy, James Schaeffer, and Charlotte S. Yeh. "Reducing Loneliness and Improving Well-being among Older Adults with Animatronic Pets." *Aging and Mental Health,* May 2, 2020, 1–7. doi.org/10.1080/13607863.2020.1758906.

Turner, Jason. "White Lion FAQ." *Global White Lion Protection Trust.* Last modified June 2018. whitelions.org/white-lion-faqs.

UlAin, Qurat, and Terry Whiting. "Is a 'Good Death' at the Time of Animal Slaughter an Essentially Contested Concept?" *Animals* 7, no. 12 (December 14, 2017): 99. doi.org/10.3390/ani7120099.

United Nations. "Global Issues: Food." un.org/en/global-issues/food.

United States Department of Agriculture Forest Service. *Wildland Fire in Ecosystems: Effects of Fire on Fauna*. Technical report no. RMRS-GTR-42-volume 1. January 2020. fs.fed. us/rm/pubs/rmrs_gtr042_1.pdf.

United States Department of Agriculture National Agricultural Statistics Service. "2017 Census of Agriculture." Table. nass. usda.gov/Quick_Stats/CDQT/chapter/1/table/1.

United States Department of Agriculture National Animal Health Emergency Management System. *NAHEMS Guidelines: Disposal*. December 2012. aphis.usda.gov/ animal_health/emergency_management/downloads/ nahems_guidelines/disposal_nahems.pdf.

USDA Animal and Plant Health Inspection Service. "Carcass Management Dashboard." U.S. Department of Agriculture. aphis.usda.gov/aphis/ourfocus/animalhealth/emergency-management/carcass-management/carcass.

USDA National Agricultural Statistics Service, *2012 Census of Agriculture - State Data*. Report no. 358. 2012. nass.usda. gov/Publications/AgCensus/2012/Full_Report/Volume_1,_ Chapter_2_US_State_Level/st99_2_011_011.pdf.

U.S. Department of the Interior National Park Service. *Handbook for the Transportation and Use of Explosives: Chapter 11 Specialized Blasting Techniques*. nps.gov/parkhistory/ online_books/npsg/explosives.

Viegas, Jennifer. "Animals Said to Have Spiritual Experiences." *NBC News*. October 8, 2010. nbcnews.com/id/wbna39574733.

Vlamis, Kelsey. "US National Parks Face 'Crisis' Over Invasive Animal Species." BBC News. Last modified December 3, 2019. bbc.com/news/science-environment-50633580.

Washington Department of Fish and Wildlife, "Roadkill Salvage Permit." wdfw.wa.gov/licenses/roadkill-salvage.

Waymarking. "Emily the Cow Grave and Animal Rights

Memorial - Sherborn." Last modified November 25, 2012. waymarking.com/waymarks/WMFT0C_Emily_the_Cow_ Grave_and_Animal_Rights_Memorial_Sherborn.

Waymarking. "Pack Animal Memorial - Skagway, AK." Last modified September 30, 2018. waymarking.com/waymarks/ WMZ8PZ_Pack_Animal_Memorial_Skagway_AK.

Ward, Ernie, Alice Oven, Ryan Bethencourt. *The Clean Pet Food Revolution: How Better Pet Food Will Change the World.* Brooklyn, NY: Lantern Books, 2020.

Water Footprint Calculator. "The 900 Gallon Diet: Meat, Portion Size and Water Footprints." watercalculator.org/ footprint/meat-portions-900-gallons.

Weaver, Caity. "What is Glitter?" *New York Times*, December 21, 2018. nytimes.com/2018/12/21/style/glitter-factory.html.

White, Tim. "Where Hogs Outnumber People by 29 to 1." *Fayetteville Observer*, April 7, 2018. fayobserver.com/ opinion/20180407/tim-white-where-hogs-outnumber-people-by-29-to-1.

Wilkinson, Gerald S. "Reciprocal food sharing in the vampire bat." *Nature* 308, no. 5955 (1984): 181–184.

Wood, Barbara A. "DOT pays dearly to have roadkill removed." *Times Herald Record* (Greenfield Park, CA), December 2010. recordonline.com/article/20000713/news/307139989.

Worden, James William. *Grief Counseling and Grief Therapy: A Handbook for the Mental Health Practitioner.* 4th ed. New York: Springer, 2009.

WorldAtlas. "What Animals Live in The Amazon Rainforest?" worldatlas.com/articles/what-animals-live-in-the-amazon-rainforest.html.

York, Tripp, and Laura Hobgood-Oster. *The End of Captivity?: A Primate's Reflections on Zoos, Conservation, and Christian Ethics.* Eugene, OR: Cascade Books, 2015.

Zhang, Sarah. "How to Get Rid of a Dead, Rotting Whale on Your Beach (Hint: Don't Blow It Up)." *Wired*. May 2, 2016. wired.com/2016/05/get-rid-dead-rotting-whale-beach-hint-dont-blow.

NOTES

[1] Hartsdale Pet Cemetery and Crematory, "War Dog Given Hero's Funeral," February 21, 2001, hartsdalepetcrematory.com/news/war-dog-given-heros-funeral.

[2] Frans de Waal, *Are We Smart Enough to Know How Smart Animals Are?* (New York: W.W. Norton & Company, 2017), 67–68.

[3] Lisa A. Kemmerer. "Verbal Activism: 'Anymal.'" *Society and Animals* 14. no. 1 (2006): 9–14.

[4] David Abram, *The Spell of the Sensuous: Perception and Language in a More-than-Human World* (New York: Vintage Books, 1996), book jacket.

[5] Melanie Joy, *Why We Love Dogs, Eat Pigs and Wear Cows: An Introduction to Carnism* (Newburyport, MA: Red Wheel, 2020), 16.

[6] For a detailed look at dogs trained to attack humans, including slavery and police contexts, see Bénédicte Boisseron's *Afro-Dog: Blackness and the Animal Question*.

[7] Robin Wall Kimmerer, *Braiding Sweetgrass* (Minneapolis: Milkweed Editions, 2015), 901.

[8] Kimmerer, *Braiding Sweetgrass*, 901.

[9] Banfield Pet Hospital, "New Survey Reveals Effects Stay-at-Home Order," *Cision: PR Newswire*. May 26, 2020. prnewswire.com/news-releases/new-survey-reveals-effects-stay-at-home-order-may-have-on-pets-and-their-owners-301064494.html.

[10] Hindu Human Rights, "Devotion of the Squirrel," June 9, 2013, hinduhumanrights.info/devotion-of-the-squirrel.

[11] Peter Harrison, "Descartes on Animals." *The Philosophical Quarterly* 42, no. 167 (1992): 219–227.

[12] Hannah Ritchie, "Livestock Outweighs Wild Mammals and Birds Ten-Fold," *Our World in Data*, April 24, 2019, ourworldindata.org/life-on-earth.

[13] Jane Goodall and Phillip L. Berman, *Reason for Hope: A Spiritual Journey* (New York: Warner, 2005), 189.

[14] Goodall and Berman, *Reason for Hope*, 189.

[15] James B. Harrod, "The Case for Chimpanzee Religion." *Journal for the Study of Religion, Nature, and Culture* 8, no. 1 (2014): 9.

[16] James B. Harrod,. "A Trans-Species Definition of Religion." *Journal for the Study of Religion, Nature, and Culture* 5, no. 3 (2011): 347.

[17] Jennifer Veigas, "Animals Said to Have Spiritual Experiences," NBC News, October 8, 2010, nbcnews.com/id/wbna39574733.

[18] Teya Brooks Pribac, *Enter the Animal: Cross-species Perspectives on Grief and Spirituality* (Sydney: Sydney University Press, 2021), 163.

[19] Brooks Pribac, *Enter the Animal*, 164.

[20] Denis Larrivee and Luis Echarte, "Contemplative Meditation and Neuroscience: Prospects for Mental Health." *Journal of Religion and Health* 57, no. 3 (2017): 960–78.

[21] Ursula King. "Interfaith Spirituality or Interspirituality? A New Phenomenon in a Postmodern World," in *Religious*

Pluralism and the Modern World (London: Palgrave Macmillan, 2012), 107–120.

[22] Wayne Teasdale, *The Mystic Heart: Discovering a Universal Spirituality in the World's Religions* (Novato, CA: New World Library, 2001), 238

[23] John Pickrell, "Oldest Known Pet Cat? 9,500-Year-Old Burial Found on Cyprus," *National Geographic*, April 8, 2004, nationalgeographic.com/animals/2004/04/oldest-known-pet-cat-9500-year-old-burial-found-on-cyprus.

[24] Although I note that the term "pet" developed from Scots/English etymology and was not used widely outside of that area until the mid-eighteenth century.

[25] Pickrell, "Oldest Known Pet Cat?"

[26] Mary Bates, "Prehistoric Puppy May Be Earliest Evidence of Pet-Human Bonding," *National Geographic*. February 26, 2018. nationalgeographic.com/news/2018/02/ancient-pet-puppy-oberkassel-stone-age-dog.

[27] Ivy D. Collier, "More Than a Bag of Bones: A History of Animal Burials," in *Mourning Animals: Rituals and Practices Surrounding Animal Death*, edited by Margo DeMello (East Lansing, MI: Michigan State University Press, 2016), 3–10.

[28] Salima Ikram. *Divine Creatures: Animal Mummies in Ancient Egypt.* (Cairo, Egypt.: American University in Cairo Press, 2015), 6.

[29] Ikram, *Divine Creatures*, 9.

[30] Ikram, *Divine Creatures*, 10.

[31] Ikram, *Divine Creatures*, 12.

[32] American Battlefield Trust, "The Cost of War: Killed, Wounded, Captured, and Missing," Civil War Casualties, accessed August 19, 2021, battlefields.org/learn/articles/civil-war-casualties.

[33] Staunton Transportation Company: J. B. Staunton, "Transportation of the Dead," The Library Company of Philadelphia, accessed August 19, 2021, digital.librarycompany. org/islandora/object/Islandora%3A6961.

[34] Livia Gershon, "A Horse's-Eye View of the Civil War," *JSTOR*, April 12, 2019, daily.jstor.org/a-horses-eye-view-of-the-civil-war.

[35] Tessa Pullan. *Civil War Horse*. United States Calvary Museum. Historical and Archaeological Society of Fort Riley, 1996. fortrileyhistoricalsociety.org/us-cavalry-museum.html.

[36] Laura Lee and Martin Lee, *Absent Friend: Coping with the Loss of a Treasured Pet* (Dorking, Surrey, UK: Ringpress, 2002), 135.

[37] Lee and Lee, *Absent Friend*, 133.

[38] Hellen R. Kemp, Nicky Jacobs, and Sandra Stewart, "The Lived Experience of Companion-animal Loss: A Systematic Review of Qualitative Studies." *Anthrozoös* 29, no. 4 (2016): 533–57.

[39] Catherine E. Amiot and Brock Bastian, "Toward a Psychology of Human–Animal Relations." *Psychological Bulletin* 141, no. 1 (2015): 6–47.

[40] Kemp, Jacobs, and Stewart, "The Lived," 533–57.

[41] Anna Chur-Hansen, "Cremation Services upon the Death of a Companion Animal: Views of Service Providers and Service Users." *Society and Animals* 19, no. 3 (2011) 248–60.

[42] Kemp, Jacobs, and Stewart, "The Lived," 533–57.

[43] Joe Sivewright and Nina Leigh Kruger, "Winning in PetCare: Pet Population," Nestlé Purina, May 7, 2019. nestle.com/sites/default/files/asset-library/documents/library/presentations/investors_events/investor-seminar-2019/petcare.pdf.

[44] Pet Food Industry, "Pet Ownership Internationally," accessed August 19, 2021, petfoodindustry.com/articles/5845-infographic-most-of-world-owns-pets-dogs-are-tops.

[45] Kunalan Manokara, et al., "Mind Your Meat: Religious

Differences in the Social Perception of Animals." *International Journal of Psychology* 56, no 3. (2020): 466–477.

[46] Gillian P. McHugo, Michael J. Dover, and David E. MacHugh, 2019, "Unlocking the Origins and Biology of Domestic Animals Using Ancient DNA and Paleogenomics." *BMC Biology* 17, doi.org/10.1186/s12915-019-0724-7.

[47] Leo Spitzer, "On the Etymology of Pet." *Language* 26, no. 4 (1950): 533.

[48] Margo DeMello, *Animals and Society: An Introduction to Human-animal Studies* (New York: Columbia University Press, 2012), 148.

[49] "Terms of Discourse." *Journal of Animal Ethics* 1, no. 1: vii–ix.

[50] PETA, "Why Animal Rights Uncompromised: 'Pets,'" accessed August 19, 2021, peta.org/about-peta/why-peta/pets.

[51] American Society for the Prevention of Cruelty to Animals, "Species Suitable to Be Companion Animals," accessed August 19, 2021, aspca.org/about-us/aspca-policy-and-position-statements/species-suitable-be-companion-animals.

[52] Sunaura Taylor, *Animal and Disability Liberation* (New York: New Press, 2017), 26.

[53] Animal Humane Society, "The Five Freedoms for Animals," accessed August 19, 2021, animalhumanesociety.org/health/five-freedoms-animals.

[54] Kirsten Persson, et al., "Philosophy of a 'Good Death' in Small Animals and Consequences for Euthanasia in Animal Law and Veterinary Practice." *Animals* 10, no 1. (2020): 124.

[55] D.J. Bartram and D. S. Baldwin, "Veterinary Surgeons and Suicide: A Structured Review of Possible Influences on Increased Risk." *Veterinary Record* 166, no. 13 (2010): 388–97.; Belinda Platt, et al., "Suicidal Behaviour and Psychosocial Problems in Veterinary Surgeons: A Systematic Review." *Social Psychiatry and Psychiatric Epidemiology* 47, no. 2 (2010): 223–40.

[56] Ernest Becker, *Denial of Death* (New York: Free Press, 1975), 26.

[57] Susana Monsó, "How to Tell If Animals Can Understand Death." *Erkenntnis*, (2019): 1–20.

[58] *ibid.*

[59] David M. Dosa, "A Day in the Life of Oscar the Cat," *New England Journal of Medicine* 357, no. 4 (2007): 328–29.

[60] Christine Morley and Jan Fook, "The Importance of Pet Loss and Some Implications for Services," *Mortality* 10, no 2. (2005): 127–43.

[61] Christopher Hall, "Bereavement Theory: Recent Developments in Our Understanding of Grief and Bereavement," *Bereavement Care* 33, no. 1 (2014): 7–14.

[62] James William Worden, *Grief Counseling and Grief Therapy: A Handbook for the Mental Health Practitioner* (New York: Springer, 2009).

[63] Liam W. Rémillard, et al., "Exploring the Grief Experience Among Callers to a Pet Loss Support Hotline," *Anthrozoös* 30, no. 1 (2017): 149-161, doi.org/10.1080/08927936.2017.1270600.

[64] Dennis Klass and Edith Steffen, *Continuing Bonds in Bereavement: New Directions for Research and Practice* (New York: Routledge, 2017), 7.

[65] Chur-Hansen, "Cremation Services upon the Death of a Companion Animal," 14–21.

[66] Becky Little, "The Environmental Toll of Cremating the Dead," *National Geographic*, November 5, 2019, nationalgeographic.com/science/2019/11/is-cremation-environmentally-friendly-heres-the-science.

[67] Peaceful Pets Aquamation, "A Closer Look: The Environmental Impact of Pet Cremation vs. Pet Aquamation,"

peacefulpetsaquamation.com/a-closer-look-the-environmental-impacts-of-pet-cremation-vs-pet-aquamation.

[68] Caity Weaver, "What is Glitter?" *New York Times*, December 21, 2018, nytimes.com/2018/12/21/style/glitter-factory.html.

[69] New York State, "Pet Cremated Remains FAQ's." *Department of State: Division of Cemeteries.* dos.ny.gov/pet-cremated-remains-frequently-asked-questions.

[70] Eric Greene, "Interview by the Author," Zoom, April 14, 2020.

[71] Rooted, "About," accessed August 19, 2021, rootedpet.com/about.

[72] Recompose, "Death-Care: Pricing," accessed August 19, 2021, recompose.life/death-care/#pricing.

[73] Daniel M. Gibbard, "Taxidermy Undergoes an Extreme Makeover," *Chicago Tribune*, March 18, 2006. chicagotribune.com/news/ct-xpm-2006-03-18-0603180240-story.html.

[74] Christina M. Colvin, "Freeze-Dried Fido: The Uncanny Aesthetics of Modern Taxidermy." In *Mourning Animals: Rituals and Practices Surrounding Animal Death*, by Margo DeMello (East Lansing, MI: Michigan State University Press, 2016), 65–71.

[75] Rifky Tkatch, et al., "Reducing Loneliness and Improving Well-being among Older Adults with Animatronic Pets," *Aging and Mental Health*, (2020): 1–7.

[76] Summum, "Modern Mummification and Transference," accessed August 19, 2021, summum.org/overview.shtml.

[77] Cryonics, "Pet Cryopreservation," accessed August 19, 2021, cryonics.org/resources/pet-cryopreservation.

[78] Richard Morgan, *Altered Carbon* (New York: Del Rey, 2018).

[79] Douglas James Davies, *Death, Ritual, and Belief: The Rhetoric of Funerary Rites* (London: Bloomsbury Academic, 2017),192.

[80] Sarah Bowen and Richard Murdoch, *Void If Detached* (Rhinebeck, NY: Teras Publishing, 2016), 373.

[81] Charles Bukowski, *The Last Night of the Earth Poems* (Santa Rosa: Black Sparrow Press, 1992), 167.

[82] Although many Gospel passages historically have been used to prop up exclusion (of Jews, "pagans," and others), I interpret these statements as saying more about the writer of the Gospel than about Jesus's teachings. This would have been a dangerous concept in a world that very much seems to be focused on distinctions of religion, gender, ethnicity, and economic status.

[83] Of interest, this story appears in all four of the Gospels (stories about the life of Jesus). That's not the case with many stories about Jesus—there's a lot of variety in what each Gospel decides to include about Jesus's actions. People usually think this story is about money. And yet, some scholars suggest it is instead about the senseless slaughter of animals used as the foundation for the temple's economy. Upon entering the temple's market, Jesus asks the merchants, "By what authority are you doing these things?" He is not specific about what the things are. But we can take a guess here, because when the story is told in another Gospel, what Jesus sees first is the animals for sale. And before he angrily flips the merchant's tables in protest, he sets those animals free. He frees the cattle, frees the sheep, and frees the doves.

[84] Jean-Loup Rault, "Be kind to others: Prosocial behaviours and their implications for animal welfare." *Applied Animal Behaviour Science* 210 (2019): 113–123.

[85] For more on helping behavior in animals, see: Connor and Norris, "Are Dolphins Reciprocal Altruists?"; Pierotti, "Spite and Altruism in Gulls"; de Waal, "Are We Smart Enough to Know How Smart Animals Are?" [apes], 67–68; Wilkinson, "Reciprocal Food Sharing in the Vampire Bat"; Hare and Kwetuenda, "Bonobos Voluntarily Share."

[86] Rault, "Be Kind to Others," 119.

[87] Inbal Ben-Ami Bartal, Jean Decety, and Peggy Mason, "Empathy and Pro-Social Behavior in Rats," *Science* 334, no. 6061 (2011): 1427–1430.

[88] Bar-On, Rob Phillips, and Ron Milo, "The biomass distribution on Earth," *Proceedings of the National Academy of Sciences* 115, no. 25 (2018): 6506–6511.

[89] WorldAtlas, "What Animals Live in The Amazon Rainforest?" accessed August 19, 2021, worldatlas.com/articles/what-animals-live-in-the-amazon-rainforest.html.

[90] Terry O'Connor. *Animals as Neighbors: The Past and Present of Commensal Species*, (East Lansing, MI: Michigan State University Press, 2013), 4–8.

[91] O'Connor, *Animals as Neighbors*, 423.

[92] O'Connor, *Animals as Neighbors*, 522.

[93] O'Connor cites Fahrig and Rytwinski 2009; Benítez-López et al. 2010; Oslowski 2008; Kociolek et al. 2010.

[94] G.E. Swan, et al., "Diclofenac Effect." *Biology Letters* 2, no. 2 (June 2006): 279–82.

[95] Gigi de Jong, "Treacherous Footing: When 122 Deer Plunge off an Icy Sierra Nevada Cliff, People Ask How Something Like This Could Happen," *Outdoor California* 80, no. 1 (2019): 36–39.

[96] de Jong, "Treacherous Footing."

[97] Lisa Levinson, "Interview with the Author," email message, May 17, 2021.

[98] National Highway Traffic Safety Association, "2020 Fatality Data Show Increased Traffic Fatalities During Pandemic," June 3, 2021, nhtsa.gov/press-releases/2020-fatality-data-show-increased-traffic-fatalities-during-pandemic.

[99] Andreas Seiler and J. O. Helldin, "Mortality in Wildlife Due to Transportation," in *The Ecology of Transportation: Managing*

Mobility for the Environment (Dordrecht, Netherlands: Springer, 2006), 165–189.

[100] Roger M. Knutson, *Flattened Fauna A Field Guide to Common Animals of Roads, Streets, and Highways* (Berkeley: Ten Speed Press, 2006), 8–9.

[101] Knutson, *Flattened Fauna*, 12.

[102] Washington Department of Fish and Wildlife, "Roadkill Salvage Permit," accessed August 19, 2021, wdfw.wa.gov/licenses/roadkill-salvage.

[103] *News Tribune*, "Dining on Roadkill: Washington Residents Gather 1,600 Deer, Elk in Law's First Year," last updated July 30, 2017, thenewstribune.com/news/local/article163842588.html.

[104] *Democrat and Chronicle*, "Seneca Park Zoo Recycles Roadkill," accessed August 19, 2021, democratandchronicle.com/story/news/2014/08/20/seneca-park-zoo-lions-deer-roadkill/14356667.

[105] Ernie Ward, Alice Oven, and Ryan Bethencourt, *The Clean Pet Food Revolution: How Better Pet Food Will Change the World* (Brooklyn, NY: Lantern Books, 2020).

[106] Joy Muller, "Interview by the Author," email message, November 27, 2020.

[107] Colvin, "Freeze-Dried Fido: The Uncanny Aesthetics of Modern Taxidermy," 65.

[108] U.S. Department of the Interior National Park Service, *Handbook: Chapter 11—Specialized Blasting Techniques*, 167–202.

[109] USDA Animal and Plant Health Inspection Service, "Carcass Management Dashboard," December 2012, aphis.usda.gov/animal_health/emergency_management/downloads/carcass-mgmt-guidelines-fao-un.pdf.

[110] Amanda Mascarelli, "Dead Whales Make for an Underwater

Feast," *Audubon*, November-December 2019, audubon.org/ magazine/november-december-2009/dead-whales-make-underwater-feast.

[111] Sarah Zhang, "How to Get Rid of a Dead, Rotting Whale on Your Beach (Hint: Don't Blow It Up)." *Wired*, May 2, 2016, wired.com/2016/05/get-rid-dead-rotting-whale-beach-hint-dont-blow.

[112] The Associated Press, "Dead Whale Brings Majestic Moments, Big Problems for Beach," *Oroville Mercury-Register*, April 27, 2016, orovillemr.com/2016/04/27/dead-whale-brings-majestic-moments-big-problems-for-beach.

[113] Alexander M. Greene, "Speaking with an Upside-Down Tongue: Reflections on Human-Elephant Multispecies Culture in Northern Thailand." *Gajah* 53 (2021): 4–19.

[114] Michael Preston, Larry Halverson, and Gayle Hesse, "Mitigation Efforts to Reduce Mammal Mortality on Roadways in Kootenay National Park, British Columbia." *Wildlife Afield* 3, no. 1 (2006): 28–38.

[115] Green Renaissance, "Highway Memorial," Vimeo, August 20, 2012, vimeo.com/47859216.

[116] Tatanka: Story of the Bison, "Kevin Costner Invites You to Visit Tatanka," accessed August 19, 2021, storyofthebison.com.

[117] Eric Grundhauser, "The Brief, Bright Life of New Zealand's Beloved Celebrity Dolphin." *Atlas Obscura*, August 22, 2017, atlasobscura.com/articles/opo-friendly-dolphin-new-zealand-opononi.

[118] Jason Turner. "White Lion FAQ," Global White Lion Protection Trust, June 2018, whitelions.org/white-lion-faqs/.

[119] Ashley A. Dayer, et al., "The Unaddressed Threat of Invasive Animals in U.S. National Parks." *Biological Invasions* 22, no. 2 (2020): 177–88.

[120] Carol Hardy Vincent, Carla N. Argueta, and Laura A.

Hanson, *Federal Land Ownership: Overview and Data. CRS Report for Congress* (2021).

[121] Kelsey Vlamis, "US National Parks Face 'Crisis' Over Invasive Animal Species," BBC News, last modified December 3, 2019, bbc.com/news/science-environment-50633580.

[122] Office of the Federal Register - U. S., 2017. Code of Federal Regulations Title 36 - *Parks, Forests, And Public Property*, (Lanham, MD: Bernan Press, 2017).

[123] Fred Pearce. *New Wild: Why Invasive Species Will Be Nature's Salvation* (Boston: Beacon Press, 2016.)

[124] Brian Handwerk, "National Zoo Deaths: 'Circle of Life' or Animal Care Concerns?" *National Geographic*, December 17, 2013, nationalgeographic.com/news/2013/12/131217-science-zoo-death-smithsonian-gazelle-hog-zebra-kudu-przewalski.

[125] Emma Marris, "Modern Zoos Are Not Worth the Moral Cost," *New York Times*, June 11, 2021.

[126] Emma Marris. *Wild Souls: How Animals Can Thrive in a Human-Made World* (London: Bloomsbury, 2021), loc 1710.

[127] Marris, "Modern Zoos."

[128] Tripp York and Laura Hobgood-Oster, *The End of Captivity?: A Primate's Reflections on Zoos, Conservation, and Christian Ethics* (Eugene, OR: Cascade Books, 2015), 9.

[129] Keri J. Cronin, *Art for Animals: Visual Culture and Animal Advocacy, 1870–1914.* (University Park, PA: Penn State University Press, 2018), 65.

[130] Caitrin Keiper. "Do Elephants Have Souls?" *The New Atlantis: A Journal of Technology & Society*, Winter/Spring 2013, thenewatlantis.com/publications/do-elephants-have-souls.

[131] Susan Reich and David Walker, "Wildlife Photographers Debate Controversial New Practices." *Photo District News* 18, no. 7 (1998): 28.

[132] Reich and Walker, "Wildlife Photographers."

[133] North American Nature Photography Association, "Truth in Captioning," August 29, 2018, nanpa.org/tag/truth-in-captioning.

[134] Reich and Walker, "Wildlife Photographers."

[135] For more on Martha: see Shufeldt, "Anatomy and Other Notes"; Cincinnati Zoo & Botanical Garden, "Passenger Pigeon Memorial"; *El Paso Morning Times*, "Last Passenger Pigeon Dies."

[136] Steven Connor, "End of the Furry Tale: The Life and Death of Knut," *Independent*, March 21, 2011, independent.co.uk/climate-change/news/end-of-the-furry-tale-the-life-and-death-of-knut-2247762.html.

[137] The Local de, "Knut's Real Fur Used for New Museum Statue," February 12, 2013, thelocal.de/20130212/47923#. USH3gasiGW9.

[138] Korea Bizwire, "Animal Memorial Ceremony Held at Seoul Grand Park Zoo," October 29, 2020, koreabizwire. com/animal-memorial-ceremony-held-at-seoul-grand-park-zoo/173237.

[139] Kiryu City, "Animal Memorial Service," Kiryugaoka Zoo, last modified October 17, 2019, city.kiryu.lg.jp.e.wt.hp.transer. com/zoo/yomoyama/1015545/1015945.html.

[140] Jason G. Goldman, "Death Rituals in the Animal Kingdom," *BBC*, September 18, 2012, bbc.com/future/article/20120919-respect-the-dead.

[141] Goldman, "Death Rituals."

[142] Cynthia Moss, *Elephant Memories: Thirteen Years in the Life of an Elephant Family* (Chicago: University of Chicago Press, 2000), 271.

[143] Keiper, "Do Elephants."

[144] Jacy Reese Anthis, *The End of Animal Farming: How Scientists, Entrepreneurs, and Activists Are Building an Animal-free Food System* (Boston: Beacon Press, 2019), ix.

[145] Anna Chur-Hansen, "Grief and Bereavement Issues and the Loss of a Companion Animal: People Living with a Companion Animal, Owners of Livestock, and Animal Support Workers," *Clinical Psychologist* 14, no. 1 (2010): 14–21.

[146] Chur-Hansen, "Grief and Bereavement Issues," 19.

[147] Jacek A. Koziel, et al., "Lab-Scale Evaluation of Aerated Burial Concept for Treatment and Emergency Disposal of Infectious Animal Carcasses," *Waste Management*, no. 76 (2018): 715–26.

[148] Silva, Aline, "Interview by the Author," Zoom, September 23, 2020.

[149] Water Footprint Calculator, "The 900 Gallon Diet: Meat, Portion Size and Water Footprints," accessed October 20, 2020, watercalculator.org/footprint/meat-portions-900-gallons.

[150] Charles Stahler, "How Many People Are Vegan? How Many Eat Vegan When Eating Out? Asks the Vegetarian Resource Group," the Vegetarian Resource Group, last modified March 2019. vrg.org/nutshell/Polls/2019_adults_veg.htm.

[151] Silva, "Interview by the Author."

[152] David L. Clough, et al., *The Christian Ethics of Farmed Animal Welfare: A Policy Framework for Churches and Christian Organizations*, CEFAW, 2020, www1.chester.ac.uk/christian-ethics-farmed-animal-welfare/cefaw-policy-framework.

[153] Clough, et al., *The Christian Ethics of Farmed Animal Welfare*, 5.

[154] Interfaith Vegan Coalition, "Coalition Members," In Defense of Animals, accessed August 19, 2021, idausa.org/campaign/sustainable-activism/interfaith-vegan-coalition/coalition-members.

[155] Interfaith Vegan Coalition, "Advocacy Kits," In Defense of Animals, accessed August 19, 2021, idausa.org/campaign/sustainable-activism/interfaith-vegan-coalition/advocacy-kits.

[156] Rancher Advocacy Program, "RAP 101," Accessed 19, 2021, rancheradvocacy.org/rap-101.

[157] American-Humane, "2014 Humane Heartland™ Farm Animal Welfare Survey."

[158] Jacy Reese Anthis, "Survey of US Attitudes Towards Animal Farming and Animal-Free Food," Sentience Institute, November 20, 2017, sentienceinstitute.org/animal-farming-attitudes-survey-2017.

[159] Jacy Reese Anthis, "Sentience Institute US Factory Farming Estimates," Sentience Institute, April 11, 2019, sentienceinstitute.org/us-factory-farming-estimates.

[160] United States Department of Agriculture National Agricultural Statistics Service, "2017 Census of Agriculture," USDA, nass.usda.gov/Quick_Stats/CDQT/chapter/1/table/1.

[161] Tim White, "Where Hogs Outnumber People by 29 to 1," *Fayetteville Observer*, April 7, 2018, fayobserver.com/opinion/20180407/tim-white-where-hogs-outnumber-people-by-29-to-1.

[162] Joy, *Why We Love*, 16.

[163] Manokara et al., "Mind Your Meat," 466–477.

[164] Charlie R. Crimston, et al., "Moral Expansiveness: Examining Variability in the Extension of the Moral World," *Journal of Personality and Social Psychology* 111, no. 4 (2016): 636–53.

[165] PETA, "Dogs in Laboratories," accessed August 19, 2021, peta.org/issues/animals-used-for-experimentation/dogs-laboratories.

[166] PETA, "Experiments on Animals: Overview," Accessed August 19, 2021, peta.org/issues/animals-used-for-experimentation/animals-used-experimentation-factsheets/animal-experiments-overview.

[167] Bruce Heller, *Gotham*.

[168] Brooks Pribac, *Enter the Animal*, 227.

[169] Anonymous, "Interview with the Author."

[170] Dharma Voices for Animals, "Right Eating: What the Buddha Taught," last modified July 9, 2014, dharmavoicesforanimals. org/eating.

[171] Dharma Voices for Animals, "Right Eating."

[172] Holly Roberts, *Vegetarian Christian Saints: Mystics, Ascetics and Monks* (San Francisco, CA: Anjeli Press, 2004).

[173] Roberts, *Vegetarian Christian Saints*, 85.

[174] United Nations, "Global Issues: Food," accessed May 17, 2021, un.org/en/global-issues/food.

[175] Qurat UlAin and Terry Whiting, "Is a 'Good Death' at the Time of Animal Slaughter an Essentially Contested Concept?" *Animals* 7, no. 12 (2017): 99.

[176] Emily Bailey, "Making Sense of Religion and Food," *Bulletin for the Study of Religion* 46, no. 2 (2017): 18–24.

[177] One study using rescue dogs in elementary education showed that "the program significantly alters students' normative beliefs about aggression, levels of empathy, and displays of violent and aggressive behavior."

[178] Lindsay Barnett, "South Korea Culls Animals on Huge Scale in Response to Foot-and-Mouth Disease, Avian Flu Outbreaks," *Los Angeles Times*, January 20, 2011, latimesblogs. latimes.com/unleashed/2011/01/south-korea-foot-mouth-disease-buries-pigs-alive.html.

[179] AP Archive, "Buddhist Ritual for Cows and Pigs Culled with Foot-and-Mouth Disease," YouTube, accessed July 30, 2015, youtube.com/watch?v=4M-QFoLbtuw.

[180] Mayumi Itoh, *The Japanese Culture of Mourning Whales: Whale Graves and Memorial Monuments in Japan* (Singapore: Palgrave Macmillan, 2018), 18.

[181] Itoh, *The Japanese Culture*, 19.

[182] Lindsey Bever. "Another Country Bans Boiling Live Lobsters as Scientists Debate Whether They Feel Pain," *Chicago Tribune*, January 13, 2018, chicagotribune.com/news/environment/ct-boiling-live-lobster-ban-20180113-story.html.

[183] Crustation Compassion, "Campaigning for the Humane Treatment of Crabs, Lobsters and Other Decapod Crustaceans in the UK," *The Voice Project*, accessed August 19, 2021, crustaceancompassion.org.uk.

[184] Atlas Obscura, "Monument in Honor of the Slaughtered Animals," Wrocław, Poland, accessed August 19, 2021, atlasobscura.com/places/monument-in-honor-of-the-slaughtered-animals.

[185] Waymarking, "Emily the Cow Grave and Animal Rights Memorial—Sherborn," last modified November 25, 2012, waymarking.com/waymarks/WMFT0C_Emily_the_Cow_Grave_and_Animal_Rights_Memorial_Sherborn.

[186] Waymarking, "Pack Animal Memorial—Skagway, AK," last modified September 30, 2018, waymarking.com/waymarks/WMZ8PZ_Pack_Animal_Memorial_Skagway_AK.

[187] Cruelty Free International, "Facts and Figures on Animal Testing," accessed August 19, 2021, crueltyfreeinternational.org/why-we-do-it/facts-and-figures-animal-testing.

[188] Suan A. Iliff, "An Additional 'R': Remembering the Animals," *ILAR Journal* 43, no. 1 (January 1, 2002): 38–47.

[189] Iliff, "An Additional," 45.

[190] Ben Panko, "This Russian Monument Honors the Humble Lab Mouse," *Smithsonian*, August 21, 2017, smithsonianmag.com/smart-news/russian-statue-honoring-laboratory-mice-gains-renewed-popularity-180964570.

[191] Dimitry Solovyov, "Georgia's Lab Apes Languish in Post-Soviet Limbo," *Reuters*, July 28, 2008, reuters.com/article/us-

georgia-monkeys/georgias-lab-apes-languish-in-post-soviet-limbo-idUKL1655341120080729.

[192] Alice George, "The Sad, Sad Story of Laika, the Space Dog, and Her One-Way Trip into Orbit," *Smithsonian Magazine*, April 11, 2018, smithsonianmag.com/smithsonian-institution/sad-story-laika-space-dog-and-her-one-way-trip-orbit-1-180968728/.

[193] Tara Gray, "A Brief History of Animals in Space," National Aeronautics and Space Administration (NASA), August 2, 2004, history.nasa.gov/animals.html.

[194] William Moy Stratton Russell and Rex Leonard Burch, *The Principles of Humane Experimental Technique* (Wheathampstead, UK: Universities Federation for Animal Welfare, 1999).

[195] Iliff, "An Additional," 39.

[196] Iliff, "An Additional," 39.

[197] Iliff, "An Additional," 44.

[198] Reese Anthis, "Sentience Institute US Factory Farming Estimates."

[199] Sailesh Rao, "Animal Agriculture Position Paper," Climate Healers (2019), https://climatehealers.org/the-science/animal-agriculture-position-paper.

ABOUT THE AUTHOR

Sarah Bowen is an animal chaplain and advocate for all creatures. She offers workshops on interspecies mindfulness practices, works with humans around animal grief/loss, and advocates for exploited and endangered species within both religious and secular contexts. You can often find her huddled over wildlife that has been struck by cars, giving each animal a sacred sendoff. Bowen is also a cofounder of Compassion Consortium, the first interfaith, interspiritual, and interspecies faith community; an academic dean at One Spirit Interfaith Seminary; a columnist on animal/human relationships for *Spirituality & Health* magazine; and the author of two award-winning books on modern spirituality, including *Spiritual Rebel*. Her work has also appeared in *Tricycle: The Buddhist Review, Elephant Journal, mindbodygreen,* and on a wide range of podcasts. She holds a BA in Human Ecology and an MA in Religious Studies and is joyfully engaged in postgraduate research in Humane Religious Studies and Anthrozoology.

Connect at modernreverend.com

Follow her on Instagram @modernreverend

REFLECTIONS